Dear Isobel

Dear Isobel

Coming to terms with the death of a child

GEORGIANA MONCKTON

WITH

HILARY BURDEN

VERMILION

LONDON

1 3 5 7 9 10 8 6 4 2

Text copyright © Georgiana Monckton 1994

The right of Georgiana Monckton to be identified as the author of this book has been asserted by her in accordance with the Copyright, Designs and Patents Act, 1988.

First published in the United Kingdom in 1994 by Vermilion
an imprint of Ebury Press
Random House
20 Vauxhall Bridge Road
London SW1V 2SA

Random House Australia (Pty) Limited
20 Alfred Street, Milsons Point, Sydney,
New South Wales 2061, Australia

Random House New Zealand Limited
18 Poland Street, Glenfield,
Auckland 10, New Zealand

Random House South Africa (Pty) Limited
PO Box 337, Bergvlei, South Africa

Random House UK Limited Reg. No. 954009

A CIP catalogue record for this book is available from the British Library

ISBN: 0 09 178137 X

Papers used by Ebury Press are natural recyclable products made from wood grown in sustainable forests.

Printed and bound in Great Britain by Clays Ltd, St Ives Plc

To all my children

Acknowledgements

We would like to thank Jennie Salkeld, Liaison Sister, Mr William Harkness, Consultant Neurosurgeon and all the staff at Great Ormond Street Hospital; Dr Christopher Baxter, Marjorie Pike and all the North London Hospice team; Dr Katherine Boodle; Revd Robert Gage and Ruth Gage; and Rebecca Glanvill, all of whom gave us tremendous support when it was needed.

The publishers would like to thank the following who supplied their services free: Slatter Anderson who designed and provided the cover artwork with the help of Prestige Couriers, Typehouse Conservatory and A One Photographic; Creative Print and Design who supplied the coverboard and printed the covers; Textype Typesetters who laid out and set the text; Magnacraft who colour separated the cover; Silverton Paper Mill and Grampian Paper who supplied the text paper.

Contents

Introduction

When Isobel was born on 19 December 1989, I remember saying to my husband Piers, 'I'll die if anything happens to my baby.' What mother doesn't think that? It's a normal, instinctive reaction when you've just given birth for the first time. Two months before her second birthday, Isobel was diagnosed with a brain-stem tumour, which proved inoperable; she died just seven weeks later.

It's now a year and a half since Isobel's death. I'm not the person I was, but I've survived. I wanted desperately to write about my experience, in the hope that it would help others to gain some knowledge about death and bereavement. This book is a personal account, based on a diary I started keeping in the lonely days after Isobel's death.

Before Isobel died, I would never have thought it necessary to read a book about bereavement. I didn't think about death. But the death of a child is so traumatic, and brings with it such unbelievably strong, such strange emotions, that what you need most is a simple explanation of what you're going through and why. You want someone to explain that such emotions are typical after a tragedy, and that you're not going mad.

It is so awful and so tragic, that you cannot begin to know how to help people who have had a child taken away from them. After all, your children are supposed to outlive you. That's why I wanted so much to write this book. Through telling my story I hope I will be able to help those people who have no experience of death, and certainly no experience of the death of a child, because so few people talk openly about such a tragedy.

Since Isobel's death I've been surprised to learn how many people have either lost a child or know a bereaved parent; if I hadn't shared my experience with them, they would never have opened up about their own. That's why I think it is important for me to say that I've had two children (with a third expected while I write) but my eldest died, whenever people ask how many children I have. That way you help others to open up. It might not feel right for everybody to say that, and of course they're entitled to their own views. Nevertheless I believe we would all feel less awkward about raising the subject of death if it were talked about more openly.

So many people I've met are uncomfortable about death because in Western society it's a taboo subject. Occasionally I've been made to feel so uncomfortable that I've actually found it difficult to tell the truth about Isobel's death. I'm sure many bereaved parents end up lying about how many children they have, which can make them feel awful, and leaves the people they meet none the wiser. So nobody learns. It's important to tell the truth and say what you think is right. There's no doubt that society needs to take more responsibility, and to open up about death. That way, losing someone you love deeply might not be as lonely and as difficult as it often is.

I've always been a very open person, but after Isobel died I felt quite alone, because there were so few people I felt I could talk to without being made to feel uncomfortable. They also had their own lives to live, and couldn't be on the phone twenty-four hours a day giving support. I needed something extra under my pillow, something I could hang on to and refer to whenever I needed to. So I went to a high-street bookshop to try and find a book I could relate to which would help me. I honestly thought I would have no trouble finding one.

I ended up having to ask where I could find a book on bereavement (I said bereavement and not child bereavement, because I thought that would be asking for the impossible). I was directed to the psychology section, where I found a handful of books written in a way that seemed to leave me feeling more confused than ever. And here was I, feeling so awful, so frightened, so in need of reassurance that I was hardly in the right frame of mind for concentrating on psychobabble. All I wanted was a detailed and simply written book about what you might expect to feel and experience when a child dies.

I discovered that a gap existed in bereavement literature. There was even less literature available on children dying between six months and twelve years of age. The books I did manage to find were on cot and neonatal deaths, but there was hardly anything to be found on what I call the 'little people' who die of either an accident or an illness. Some of the books were helpful, but only in particular areas. In the main they were not written in enough detail, and most of them were not written first-hand. I couldn't find a book which suited what I needed. I didn't need a psychological analysis of what I was going through. I needed an honest, first-person account, and so it occurred to me that I should write my own.

I believe that if there was more written about bereavement it would not be the closed subject that it is

now. There are plenty of books about romance, or on
crime – why not on death and how to cope with it?
After all, it happens to all of us. But we're brought up to
not talk about death. Many families now talk about
most things in life, whether it's birth, periods, sex, or
marriage, but death is very rarely mentioned until it
happens, like it did to us. Then we were totally unprepared.

I will never be the same again. It's true that when you
lose a child, a part of you dies. I feel as if I have a leg or
arm missing. Most of us are very quick to say that life
goes on – too quick. Of course life goes on, but you've
also got to grieve. Even after the initial grieving is over
and the pain has subsided a little, you will never get
over it totally, although you will learn to live with your
loss.

If bereavement was made less scary, less taboo, and
more a part of life (which it is, after all), I think we
would be better able to keep the spirit of a dead person
alive. To me that's very important. I'm not saying that
you should lay a place at dinner for them, or that you
should bring them up in every conversation you have.
You do have to let go. But you have to let go in a very
special way. Although many of us use the phrase 'let
go', 'coming to terms' is, I think, more appropriate. I
told myself that I was never going to let go; Isobel was
always going to be my oldest daughter, she was always
going to be Isobel, she would always be included. What
you 'let go' of is the thought that they might come
back. That is what coming to terms with death is, and
you can only do that in your own time. For some people
it may take years.

It's important to be able to feel that you can grieve
and get on with life with ease, and not be made to feel
uncomfortable or out of the ordinary. You are made to

feel uncomfortable because death and grief are taboo, and they are taboo subjects because there's little written about them, and not enough open discussion. It's a vicious circle. If they were more open subjects people would be more able to cope. Of course grief is also private, but at the same time it should be a subject that children and adults learn about, instead of one that is shut away, a denial, and as if nothing has happened.

Of course my experience is not the same as everyone's; we all experience grief in a unique way. But I hope people will be able to find something helpful in this book, either for themselves or for someone they know. I'm writing it from my own experience. Readers must pick out for themselves as much or as little as they find comforting or helpful. I want to make something that is going to happen to everyone of us a subject that we should not be ashamed to talk about. I want to explain bereavement in a way that is honest and natural. I want people to know what a tragic loss does to people, and how they cope with that for the rest of their lives. And more than anything I want to express my belief that death isn't as frightening as people think it is: it can be a pathway to somewhere else, and not such a final ending after all.

SUMMER 1991

Chapter One

I have always loved children. Before I had Isobel I was a Montessori teacher, and I suppose my life was always geared towards the under five-year-olds. Their absolute innocence, so rare in adults, enthralled me. I was naturally drawn to that side of their nature, and I was at my happiest when I had children running around me. It gave me enormous satisfaction when I taught three letters to a child who said them back to me a week later. I got my own reward for that, so it was only natural when I married Piers to want to start a family almost straight away.

Luckily I had no trouble in conceiving, but I had to give up teaching very early in my pregnancy because I suffered terribly from nausea all day. As a result, my whole mind was geared towards this little person growing inside me. Like any new mum I was apprehensive about suddenly having such a huge responsibility. I found it very stressful. I was even more worried when Isobel was born a little prematurely. It was quite a shock for me, and made me all the more aware of how precious she was. My love for her was so intense it hurt. I'm sure every mother looks at her new baby and thinks, 'My God, how amazing, I made that little person.' She had my whole attention, and she was always at the top of my list of priorities.

I remember in hospital when she was taken away from me for twenty-four hours to the special care unit. I was trying to feed her myself, but because she was so small she wasn't really sucking properly. I remember expressing milk for her, running down the hospital corridor with a jar of expressed milk. My heart collapsed to see her tiny little body in an incubator, dressed in a bright blue baby-gro and with a tube up her nose. She wasn't eating, because she had jaundice very badly. As part of her treatment she spent hours under a sunlamp with nothing on except goggles. To a new mum nothing could be worse than seeing your baby in that condition. She was just three days old.

To me, she was always a special little baby. I was absolutely petrified of her to be honest; I just didn't know what to do with her. In a way because I was so nervous of her, and because she knew nothing and depended on me, the two of us were able to grow together. I gained love for her and grew in confidence while she was growing to love me. I was fiercely protective of her. She was mine, and she was my first. I was quite young, twenty-five, and I'd only been married for eighteen months, so the whole experience was quite bewildering. The slightest little thing that was wrong with her and I went straight to the doctor. No one can ever quite prepare you for parenthood.

Isobel was a very well behaved baby, full of happiness that drew people to her. She had the most beautiful eyes, and the darkest, longest eyelashes. I used to think she'd never have to wear mascara, and that her eyebrows were so well-shaped she'd never have to pluck them. She loved going to see cows and horses. One of the first noises she made was a moo – cats went moo, dogs went moo, everything went moo.

One day, when Isobel was about a year old, we were out walking in the cold wind and I noticed her eye tearing. It wasn't red, there was just a single tear coming from her right eye. I didn't think anything of it, until a couple of months later the same eye began to 'goo'. The doctor told me it was conjunctivitis, and gave her eye drops which seemed to help for three or four weeks. Then the gooey eye came back. Her tear duct was blocked, and I was told to massage the side of her nose from time to time to help it unblock. By this time, I was pregnant with Emily.

During the summer I made an appointment for Isobel to see an eye specialist, but her eye cleared up again so I cancelled it. Of course, as soon as I'd done that, her gooey eye came back again.

Emily was born on 29 August. I always wanted a close age gap. Ideally, I wanted it to be two years, but I conceived very quickly again. This was lucky, as it happened, because it gave Isobel and Emily some time together. It was an easy birth, and Emily was healthy, except for a slight eye condition called ptosis which I wasn't told about until after Isobel had died. (Emily will have to have two eye operations when she is three to correct the condition.) I bought Isobel a little nurse's uniform so that when she came to see me in hospital she'd feel a part of everything and look like the other nurses. She was as good as gold and absolutely riveted. I don't know if Isobel understood I was having a baby. I think Piers and I underestimated her powers of understanding because she couldn't talk.

When we came home, Isobel was very caring but sometimes clumsy with Emily. All she wanted to do was give her a hug, but sometimes she'd fall on her accidentally. We didn't know it then, but the tumour was obviously making her lose control. The more I think about it now, the more pictures I look at from that summer, the more you can see she was ill. And yet we were living in ignorance. Maybe it was a blessing in disguise, because when we did eventually find out it meant we only had seven weeks of torture.

Isobel's eye became worse than ever, so I took her to see the eye specialist. He said her tearduct needed to be unblocked, so we made an appointment at Moorfield's Eye Hospital for 4 October. Although it was only a very minor operation, it was very stressful to us. She had to be absolutely still, so they gave her a general anaesthetic.

I went to the operating theatre with her. I'd never been into an operating theatre before without being the patient. I had to wear green overalls, a hat and mask. Poor Isobel didn't know what was going on. They put a huge gas mask over her face and all I could see were these big, bright eyes peering over the mask. I'd just had Emily and felt very emotional seeing Isobel like that. She fought the gas and it took a long time to take effect. Eventually she went under; her tearduct was cleared, she came round and after a couple of hours we were allowed to take her home. Everything seemed just fine, and we were hopeful that would be the end of it.

Later that week, Piers took me out to dinner. I was on top of the world. I remember saying to him, 'Aren't we lucky? We've got two beautiful daughters, and I feel wonderful.' At that moment, our lives seemed perfect. Piers was about to turn twenty-nine, and I was in the process of organising a surprise birthday party for him. It turned out to be a great success, soon irrelevant and forgotten, when twenty-four hours later, our lives were turned completely upside down. We hadn't planned it that way, but we entered this drama as strong as we could have ever been.

Chapter Two

On Sunday, 20 October 1991, just after Piers' birthday party, Isobel was being unusually difficult. We were out walking. Emily was only seven weeks old and due for a feed, so we left her at home with our mother's help, Rebecca. Isobel decided she was happier being carried, but when I picked her up she wanted to be put down again. She couldn't make up her mind what she wanted. Her wellington boot kept falling off the same foot. Nothing to worry about, we thought, but overnight she became much worse. The next day she began walking with a swinging gait, almost as if she'd had a stroke, though she wasn't in any pain. That's when I first realised things were not at all right.

Within a matter of hours, she started to stumble noticeably and fall over quite a lot. We then realised she wasn't using her right hand to feed herself, which was unusual. She was also experiencing massive mood swings, which I'd previously put down to jealousy over Emily. Her eye was green with goo again, and I thought it must be something to do with that. We took her to our local GP, Dr Katherine Boodle, and within minutes three or four doctors were looking at her. They watched her walking, and she was limping so badly it was almost embarrassing that I hadn't noticed it before. It was heartrending to watch. They laid her down, and felt the temperature of her legs; her right leg was like ice, which I'd never noticed before.

We went home and waited that afternoon while they decided what the next move would be. A call came through at about 4 pm. Piers answered and when he put the telephone down, he looked at me with fear in his eyes. I asked him who it was. He said, 'Darling, Isobel has to go into Barnet General for three days of tests.' That's when the first alarm bells rang. Oddly enough, I wasn't so worried about the tests. I was more worried about the three days, how Isobel would be able to sleep at night and whether or not I could be with her. Looking back, these should have been the least of my worries.

That evening, I'd just put Isobel to bed when our GP popped in to see us. She sat down and tried to calm and comfort us. There wasn't a lot she could say, but she was desperately trying to keep the conversation positive. She knew there was something seriously wrong, but there was no way she could tell us what at this stage.

The next day we took Isobel to Barnet General. Luckily I didn't need to worry about Emily, because I trusted Rebecca and I wasn't breast-feeding. If I hadn't had someone as competent, or if I'd had to get someone in, I would have had Emily as well as Isobel to worry about.

Isobel had a CAT scan immediately after the paediatrician had examined her, which meant they had to sedate her to keep her still. She had a needle put in her hand and she just hated it. She was looking at me – I'll always remember that look in her eyes – as if to say, 'Mummy, what is going on, why are you letting these people do this to me?' I had no idea that it was going to be as bad as it was. I just thought she had a virus. It was nature, I think, protecting me. Piers knew, though. He knew something was seriously the matter, but he hid his feelings to protect me.

Piers, my mother and I were shown into a cubicle while we waited for the results. A cot was provided for Isobel, and we sat eating sandwiches for lunch, trying to act normally. After a couple of long hours, the paediatrician came in. I will never, ever forget his face. He told us they'd found a 'growth' in Isobel's brain. I glanced from my husband to my mother, with growing unease, while both looked distraught. They understood immediately that Isobel's life was in danger, and tears began to well up in their eyes.

All I remember is rushing out of that cubicle and down the ward, crying uncontrollably, Mummy rushing after me. I remember standing at the top of the stairs screaming, 'Mummy, she's not going to die, is she? Is she?' I could hear my voice echoing down the stairwell and a few people were staring at me, with pity in their eyes. I was in a complete state of panic; the release button had been pushed for a couple of minutes. Then I pulled myself together again. It was as if nature had let me in a bit. Then I *had* to be all right. Of course I couldn't let Isobel know.

We had sometimes wondered why she couldn't talk properly. Maybe it was the tumour. She was a very intelligent little girl. From the age of fourteen months she understood everything. She was full of double dutch, very vocal, but all she was ever really able to say was 'Mummy' and 'Daddy'; even those words were slurred. She didn't have to say anything about what was going on. It was in her eyes. We'd also wondered about her behaviour with little Emily – how she would go up to her and fall on her. Of course, all she was trying to do was kiss her, but the tumour was making her clumsy.

Because we now knew there was something wrong with Isobel we started noticing all the signs. She was getting worse by the minute, deteriorating physically. I couldn't even let go of her in the ward playroom without her falling over. I could see the paralysis down one side of her body, the very slight droop, and the dribbling just on one side of her mouth. Either we'd simply not noticed before, or maybe the tumour had started taking a grip and this was the first bite. Both Piers and I felt totally numb.

Chapter Three

We arrived at Great Ormond Street Hospital that same evening, already exhausted. We went into what was going to be Isobel's home for the next two weeks, Ward 1B, and my first thought was, 'My God, how on earth is she going to get any sleep?' You couldn't swing a cat. Having said that, although it was very crowded you could sense an atmosphere full of life and support. There was a wealth of feeling in that ward, an almost indescribable bond.

We went through another three or four hours of questioning from doctors. Isobel was extremely tired. She had more tests. I realised they had to get things moving, but all I really wanted was for them to leave us alone, let Isobel sleep and do everything the next day. At this stage, anyone who wore a stethoscope around their neck, or nurse's uniform felt the wrath of Isobel's lungs. At around midnight, Isobel finally went to sleep. I was completely drained. Piers went home to get what sleep he could, and I was left on my own for the first time since all this had happened. Although there were lots of people around, I suddenly felt totally alone.

I went and sat in the big television room where two other mothers were sitting talking. They told me both their children had cancer and they'd been at Great Ormond Street for six months. I found talking to them amazingly comforting, and they knew exactly what I was going through. I couldn't believe how well they were coping, but they just had to. They'd come to accept it as a way of life. The only difference between us was that some had more hope than others, which I didn't know at the time.

I went to the parents' room on the fifth floor, five minutes from Ward 1B. Three other mothers were fast asleep, and I fumbled around in the dark trying to find the ladder to my bunk. I was feeling pretty wretched with a cold, and I lay there, dazed, frightened, confused, unable to sleep. It was like a bad dream – I didn't realise why I was there. A curious numbness comes over you, perhaps it's nature's way of protecting you. I refused to contemplate any possibility other than that Isobel was going to get better.

I found it terribly difficult to switch off. Eventually I took a dose of Night Nurse to help me get a few hours' sleep, which I thought I would need. I knew if there was trouble with Isobel downstairs the nurses would come and wake me. I managed to get a couple of hours' sleep and woke up at about 4 am. I went down to the ward to see Isobel for reassurance and had a cup of tea with the nurses. We had a chat about nothing in particular; I think they were trying to take my mind off Isobel, who was sleeping. I stayed there for about an hour, and went back up to get some more sleep. I was back in the ward by 7 am, by which time Isobel had woken up.

We were then given a second opinion on the CAT scan. We were told it was a tumour, but partly cystic. I didn't really understand, but I thought that the fact that they were saying cyst – which I thought was like a blister – meant it couldn't be that bad.

That day Isobel had an MRI scan, which produces a far more detailed image. Before she had the general anaesthetic she wasn't allowed to have anything to eat or drink. I had to entertain her for what seemed like ages before they were able to fit Isobel in for the scan, although it was only a couple of hours. She was tired, irritable, thirsty and didn't know what was going on. I had to try to keep her mind off needing a drink. She wouldn't be put down and she was looking at me with such terrified eyes. This turned out to be an introduction to her behaviour to come. She wouldn't go to anyone but me; even when I darted off to the loo leaving her in Piers' arms, I'd hear her screaming after me. Finally she went to have her scan. I went home for the first time to catch up on some sleep, while Piers went down with Isobel. The results came through that evening, and they showed very clearly a tumour with a small cyst in her brain stem.

Isobel was deteriorating in front of our eyes. She was very moody, clingy, and in a lot of pain. The fluid in the cyst was causing swelling and exerting pressure on her brain, so that was the reason for all the symptoms we now realised were abnormal. They were going to operate to try to remove some of the tumour, and send it to the laboratory for analysis.

We expected to have to wait a week for the operation. That was very hard because we felt so helpless. I hated to see her in this way and I wanted them to do something for her straight away. There was nothing we could do but pace up and down the hospital with her, drawing her attention to pictures on the wall, trying to distract her. There was a tiny playroom with loads of toys and a wonderful Wendy house which she absolutely adored. She'd limp in and hang out of the window, waving to us.

What struck me was just how seriously ill the children in Great Ormond Street were. After a couple of days we became like one big family. There was very much a feel-

ing of being in it together. I couldn't believe the
strength I had. I hadn't done a great deal with my life,
and I suppose I wasn't very worldly, but somehow I
coped. If I thought I was going to burst out crying, I
passed Isobel to Piers. I didn't want her to see me break-
ing down – I thought that was important. More often
than not, though, I kept on going. I used to visit a little
chapel in the hospital. I remember being so angry at
God, so angry. I couldn't understand, if there was a
God, why He made children suffer in this way. I prayed
time after time for Him to make Isobel live, and I
couldn't understand why He wouldn't listen.

While we were waiting for the operation, Piers suggested we take Isobel out for the day to give her a break.
The hospital thought it would be a good idea; she
seemed to be levelling out, and her symptoms were
improving thanks to the steroids she was given to
reduce the pressure on her brain from the tumour. We
decided to take her to London Zoo. We had to park the
car miles away from the gates, which was a bad start
because she didn't want to be put in her pushchair due
to her condition. She was clingy, and who could blame
her? So I carried her all the way. She was so heavy, but
she wouldn't go to Piers, and I started thinking it hadn't
been such a good idea.

We got to the Zoo. Isobel always loved animals, and
we thought it would be the best thing for her to be surrounded by them. Well, it worked the opposite way. She
just wasn't interested, and she obviously felt appalling.
She was on steroids, which were making her hungry.
Isobel was so pale, people were looking at her wondering what was wrong. We sat in the open cafeteria and
while Piers was queuing for food for Isobel, I sat with
her on my lap and it finally sank in how ill she was. I
looked at the other children around us and they all

looked so normal compared to Isobel. We'd grown used to her appearance, and hadn't realised how dreadful she really looked. She couldn't or wouldn't walk, and when she started twitching I just turned to Piers and said, 'Please, let's get out of here.' It was one of the unhappiest days of my life.

In the end the operation was brought forward because she was declining so quickly. As the days went by, you could see that the tumour was taking over her behaviour. Being with her was like playing charades, continual guesswork about what she wanted because her brain was muddling and irritating her. I couldn't put her down; she wouldn't leave me. This got worse and worse and was terribly hard on Piers because Isobel didn't want to go to him at all. So he tended to put everything on my shoulders; it was always up to me to make sure that Isobel got enough sleep. If I lost my temper or was slightly agitated with Isobel out of sheer exhaustion or emotional tension, he would jump down my throat. I was doing everything I possibly could, and it seemed so unfair.

Piers and I were shown photographs of what Isobel would probably look like after the operation to prepare us for the shock and to familiarise us with the hospital equipment. There was a possibility she would come out wired up to a ventilator which would do her breathing for her. After seeing her safely into the theatre, we were advised to leave the hospital and to go and do something completely different to take our minds off everything for a while. We went to an Italian restaurant and tried to eat lunch. Afterwards, would you believe, I went and had my legs waxed. I remember telling the beautician what was going on. Of course she didn't know what to say or do, but I had to get it off my chest.

The hospital had told us to check in at regular inter-

vals to see what was happening. Finally, after seven
hours they said she was on her way up from theatre. I
couldn't understand why it had taken so long, but we
soon found out that despite trying his hardest, the sur-
geon couldn't remove any of it, except a tiny piece for
the analysis biopsy. All he could do was drain the cyst
which had formed around the tumour and take some
of the pressure off her brain. The tumour was malignant. It was an enormous blow.

Brain-stem tumours are very, very rare. In Britain,
only six children a year of Isobel's age get them. The
surgeons found that the tumour was the size of a grape,
and highly aggressive. The brain stem controls everything that is essential for sustaining life. The tumour
was, therefore, inoperable. Even if it had been benign,
they couldn't have taken much out because it would
have left her severely brain damaged at best. It had
taken all that time to do what they did safely, without
damaging her any further. The actual tumour was inter-
meshed with all her brain tissue.

We went in to see her so that we could be there when
she came round. Although I'd mentally braced myself
beforehand, seeing her just about destroyed me. But I
was still numb; even now when I think of it, it doesn't
seem real somehow. She had a huge bandage on her
head. It was quite a small room, and her little figure was
overwhelmed by hospital machinery. I was terribly
frightened. Basically, her prognosis had been poor
from the time we walked into Great Ormond Street, but
it took a long time for the realisation to sink in. When
William Harkness (the paediatric neurosurgeon) came
in to tell us she only had weeks to live, I said to him,
'You never know, miracles do happen.' I wasn't going to
give up on her. I had a terrible, sick feeling in my stom-
ach. What he told us was disastrous news but I was so

numb with shock that I didn't shed a tear.

Thirty-six hours after the operation she was actually
out of bed playing. The internal swelling started going
down, and to our amazement she began to talk. She
recognised Bambi on the wall and tried to say his name
– it wasn't quite right, but she was actually talking! She
was such a strong little girl. I'll always remember holding her for the first time just after the operation. She
was critically ill, yet still wanting to be hugged. Gently I
lifted her out of her cot and just held her. It was wonderful, but at the same time I couldn't believe that here
I was, holding such a seriously sick little girl. She'd gone
through all the tests and the operation – for nothing.
The love I felt for her was so strong I thought my heart
would break in two.

Chapter Four

Piers and I still had one more decision to make. There were other treatments on offer: chemotherapy and radiotherapy; but even with these there was only a slight chance of Isobel surviving, and an even smaller chance of her surviving with her mental and physical abilities unimpaired. We could choose, but I knew. I didn't have to think. I thought it was nature's way of saying she was not meant to be here. Piers took a lot longer to decide. He wanted to hold on to the hope that something might cure her. All I wanted was to bring her home.

I was pleased it was malignant. That may sound dreadfully callous, but if it had been benign, I couldn't have watched my child go through chemotherapy and radiotherapy simply to prolong her life just a little. I just knew we had to let her go. Meanwhile there was poor little Emily, our second-born. She was only seven weeks old and of course I hadn't really got to know her, because I was giving all my attention to Isobel.

Thankfully, once Isobel had recovered from the operation we were allowed to take her home to live what little life she had left. Jennie, the liaison sister assigned to us from Great Ormond Street, sat us down and told us what was going to happen, how we might feel, what Isobel's symptoms could be, what medication she would be on, and how she would be there for us, along with the North London hospice team and our GP, Dr Boodle. Once or twice I noticed an odd thing when I talked to Dr Boodle about Isobel's condition and how I felt. I found myself smiling, although I was feeling so desperate. Somehow, for some reason, I couldn't help myself. She didn't flicker, she accepted it, so I thought it must have been a normal, nervous reaction.

Piers had to go back to work. He'd missed a lot but it was a tremendous relief to us that his boss had been sympathetic; his job wasn't threatened by all the time off he'd had to take. That left me with the responsibility of looking after Isobel. I was very lucky to have an enormous amount of support. Our GP, Jennie and the hospice team were in constant touch. My mother was around, as well as Rebecca and Piers' mother, who visited frequently, so I was able to concentrate on Isobel while they did the shopping and cooking. I wanted to spend every second I had with my little girl. Piers and I were less tense together during this period. The last thing we needed was a bad atmosphere at home – we just had to get on with it.

With the pressure gone from her brain, Isobel seemed much better. She was able to walk more easily and had regained her appetite. She was the most normal I'd seen her for a couple of weeks, and I suppose that set me thinking that she was going to get better.

Isobel had been back at home for a few days when some very good friends came to visit. After lunch we all went for a walk. We didn't even manage to get to the end of the front footpath before she became very irritable. Poor Isobel's brain just wasn't letting her function properly. I remember feeling a little embarrassed for our friends, who hadn't realised how bad the situation

was and didn't really understand. To see Isobel like this
unnerved them, and made them feel uncomfortable.
The next day, she was already struggling to walk and
keep her balance and Calpol was being given to her regularly. That's when I heard about the faithhealer.

It was one of Isobel's godmothers who told me about
a particular faithhealer who had cured someone with
cancer. At that point, I was willing to try anything, even
though we'd been told there was nothing anybody
could do. We were going to go to any lengths, to try
everything possible. I wanted to put every positive
thought I had into Isobel.

I rang the faithhealer and pleaded with her to help
my dying daughter. She asked me to tell her about Isobel, to tell her what had happened, and how I was feeling. I told her she had a brain-stem tumour, and that
they'd done everything they could in the hospital; what
we had to look out for now was the pressure on her
brain causing irritation and pain. I know some people
find this hard to believe, but over the telephone she
said she could actually see the swelling in Isobel's brain
and that she would start working on her straight away.

The next day I saw a dramatic change in Isobel. Her
walking was improving, with the help of some ankle
boots which gave her support, and she didn't seem to
need any Calpol. The faithhealer stayed in contact by
telephone until one day she came to see us. She was an
amazing lady, and had an extraordinary way with Isobel. She had this incredible power. With Isobel sitting
on my lap the faithhealer would massage her bad leg,
the side that was paralysed, and Isobel would just lie
there quietly. After a while you could feel a tremendous
heat from the healer's hands, and more often than not
Isobel would get quite drowsy. Thanks to that incredible lady, Isobel had two wonderful weeks when she was

relatively pain-free and happy. She had more strength in her walk, but was still limping. I can see her dragging that leg down the passage even now, but she used to laugh about it . She would look at her leg and giggle; she couldn't understand why she walking in such a funny way.

Isobel adored Emily and tried to be so gentle with her. Those couple of weeks were the only time they really had together as sisters. Isobel would help feed her, as clumsy as she was. She'd kiss Emily and Emily would gurgle, oblivious to how ill her big sister was.

Isobel also started to use her right hand more, and actually sat and drew some pictures. She licked some stars and pressed them onto sheets of paper, and drew a few squiggles. She held the pen perfectly, with total control – I was amazed. I wrote the date on the bottom of her drawings. It was 22 November, just three weeks before she died. (We've since framed them and have them in the playroom.)

I was convinced that the faithhealer was helping Isobel, and despite everything, I still believed that she was going to get better. I was hanging on to the idea that a miracle would save her and refused to believe she was going to die. I even told our GP she was getting better. I could see on the doctors' faces that they didn't believe me, but when you are desperate you will do anything to make your child live.

One evening some very good friends of ours suggested we get out for an evening, leave Rebecca to look after Isobel, and go out with them to a cheap Italian restaurant. They thought it would take our minds off what was happening just for a couple of hours. I felt that it was a good idea, but as we sat waiting for our food everyone, even Piers, was deliberately not mentioning Isobel. I sat at the table, tears in my eyes, a lump in my throat. I couldn't pretend: my child was gravely ill, and was going to die at some point in the near future. The finality of it hit me, and I suddenly became aware that these might be her last days.

At the hospital Isobel had lived in pyjamas and had no real routine. I decided I'd try to give her a sense of day and night again to get her back to the routine she had before she was ill. Even during those well days, she would sit on my lap quite a lot, nodding off occasionally.

Because she seemed to be in such unexpectedly good form I decided to take her to Sainsbury's. I thought it would do her good to get out of the house and to have some normality back in her life. I put her in the shopping trolley and it felt just like old times. I got to the checkout, and all of a sudden, Isobel started to change. You could almost see the tumour eating her, grabbing at her. I quickly got her out of the trolley. She was grabbing at my face and pulling my hair. People were beginning to look. I had to say to the shop assistant, that I was sorry, that my child was very ill. At the same time I desperately wanted to tell people she was dying. No one helped me. I guess she looked like a badly behaved two-year-old. That was the last time Isobel ever went out. It was also one of the last days I was able to give her a proper bath.

We had tried to keep bathing her every day. I started noticing how thin she was getting, and how motionless. Sometimes I'd lift her out of the bath and she would just lie there, waiting to be dried. Her eyes would close and she'd fall asleep while I was dressing her. Sometimes she'd open her big blue eyes and smile at me before going back to sleep. There's one special moment I will always remember, because Isobel almost hypnotised me. It sounds crazy, but she made me look at her, without saying anything. We had direct eye-to-eye contact for about a minute. I was oblivious to anything or anyone else. She was actually saying to me, it was written in her eyes: 'Mum, don't worry. I know what's going to happen. I really do know. I know I'm going to leave you, I know I'm going to leave everybody, and I know I'm going to die, but I'm going to be all right.' It was a very special moment, and then it was gone. She went back to doing something else.

She knew she was ill and going to die, although she never lost the will to live and wanted to make a fight of it because she didn't want to leave us. I never talked to her about being ill – I decided there was no point. She couldn't respond, so there was no way of telling if it would have had the desired effect. Of course when she was in pain, or having a drip put in, her eyes would dart to me and she would want soothing words from me. But otherwise everything was kept as normal as possible, and I tried to keep the worry in my eyes away from her.

As she grew worse, she wanted to rest in the morning and afternoon, and so I put her in her cot. As the days went by, and she was getting sleepier, she began to spend most of her days in the playroom. We stopped giving her rests in her cot, and just let her catnap on the red beanbag, or on our laps. By this time, she was in far more pain and was put on codeine and valium. I had to wake her up every four hours to give her pain relief. We were constantly in touch with the hospice team about pain relief, and with the faithhealer by telephone. One day the hospice doctor came to visit her, and there were tears in his eyes. I said: 'She hasn't got long, has she?' He said he thought she had about two weeks. I telephoned Piers and told him she was going downhill fast and that he ought to stop work, to please stay home and make the most of the time she had left.

When Piers stopped work his support was amazing. I was very proud of him for doing one thing in particular, although I wish we had not had to go through it at all. We had two suppositories of high doses of valium, just in case she went through the pain barrier or had a fit. The brain stem is so narrow that any change in the tumour would have increased her pain. One day we were sitting in the playroom, watching the leaves falling from the trees outside. Isobel started to twitch slightly. It was obvious that the tumour was changing; it happened so quickly. Suddenly she was in such pain, her brain was experiencing such irritation; it was awful to watch. She didn't know what she wanted, and she started to shake. I had to hold her on my lap as hard as I could to stop her from thrashing around. Piers rushed upstairs and got one of the suppositories. We laid her down on the floor, and it took three of us to hold down her little body. For Piers to be so calm, to remember what we were told to do by the doctors, and to insert a suppository up her bottom, impressed me greatly.

Towards the end, Isobel needed constant pain relief, so she was put on a drip of morphine and valium, which made her sleepier and sleepier. The drip made it awkward to change her pyjamas, and we could no longer bath her. Instead I sponged her down. From that point on she was hardly aware of her physical surroundings.

The faithhealer was in touch with us, and did her utmost to reverse the tumour but she couldn't manage it. Isobel started going downhill; the faithhealer realised that nothing could be done, so she resolved instead to make Isobel as comfortable as possible. We'll never know if she was able to do that, although I'm sure Isobel was as peaceful as she could have been. I like to think it was because of the faithhealer. Isobel slept for most of the day on her bright red beanbag, but I'm sure she was still aware of what was going on around her. Very occasionally she'd open her eyes and then go back to sleep again.

The only emotion she experienced before she was ill was love. There was no suffering. She died without knowing the meaning of hurt, or anger, arrogance or selfishness, and in that respect you could say she was lucky. The faithhealer tried with all her might to do what she could for Isobel, and we will always be grateful to her.

As a parent, you naturally map out your child's life. You wonder what they're going to look like, who they might marry, what they're going to do with their life, who they're going to take after. You're constantly looking into the future. But in those few hours when we were told our child wasn't going to live, everything we'd imagined and hoped for – her future – was destroyed. It is such a shock that it is no wonder you change as people: you never see life as that rosy again.

Piers and I hardly noticed each other's company, because we were so busy with Isobel and making sure Emily got love and comfort as well. We didn't have the mental stamina to console one another, and the atmosphere between us was increasingly tense. There were countless times when we were just too exhausted and emotionally drained even to communicate. We were watching our child, whom we both loved passionately, die.

WINTER 1991

Chapter Five

On Sunday 8 December, Isobel lost consciousness. We had no idea how close she was to dying – probably just days. She was very white, but she looked beautiful, her skin was so clear and flawless. Her pulse was very weak and her breathing was erratic. At that age, you're meant to breathe around twenty-seven breaths a minute. She was taking maybe ten or eleven breaths a minute. We thought she was dying. I was distraught. This was our very first glimpse of death. We sat there holding her. The vicar came and said a prayer. I was crying my eyes out. Until this time I'd only been taking one day at a time.

Ten minutes later, she woke up, gave me a smile, and her breathing returned to normal. She even tried to get up and walk out of the room. She managed it, with my help. That was the first time she'd walked for weeks. It was as if she was saying, 'I'm not going to die yet. I'm not going to leave you. I'm not ready.'

I wanted to be there holding her when she died, and I wanted her to die soon because it was so painful to watch her struggling. She would get so close, so close to death, and then she'd pick herself up again. It made it harder for me knowing that she didn't want to go. This went on all week. The hospice doctor and nurses visited Isobel every day. Each time they would leave believing they would never see her again. Isobel went for four days without food or drink. The only thing we could do for her was to use the little sticks we'd been given; they had a tiny sponge on the end which we dipped in water and used to wipe her mouth. That was all she had, apart from the morphine and valium doses which were increasing by the day. She was having very high doses of pain relief for such a little body. The fact that she tolerated it showed her strength. She didn't want to give up, and that tore our hearts even more.

We started to suspect that the faithhealer was still tuned in to Isobel, that perhaps it was her concentration keeping her alive. I rang her and told her that Isobel was not dying, that she wouldn't let go and that we all wanted her to let go. It was becoming too much for us. Isobel would drain completely, she would go grey, we'd think that was it – and then she would pick up again. After my telephone call to the faithhealer, I knew she was going to stop working on her.

The following Sunday, Isobel was so peaceful. We were told on the Friday that she would probably die that weekend. It was nearing Christmas, so we rushed out to get a little tree. She still managed to open her eyes and look at that tree and try to touch it. She had her first glimpse of Christmas with the lights, so that was nice. There was a sense of, 'All right, okay, I've had enough, I'm going.'

At a quarter to eight that evening she started to drain; everything was shutting down. She went whiter and whiter. I just held her, and her breathing got worse and worse. It was painful to watch because she was making a coarse, choking sound, almost frog-like, as if she wasn't getting enough air. It sounded so painful, but apparently it isn't; it's a part of dying. It was so loud, it tore me to pieces.

In the end I was saying, 'Please let go, just let go.' We watched videos with her, *Mary Poppins* and *The Little Mermaid*. Apparently the last sense to go is hearing, so we kept playing videos and hoped she could hear us talking. We wanted to say so many things and I wished she would squeeze my hands like you see in the films, but she didn't. She was so ill, but she was a fighter, such a strong little girl with a lot of will to live. She was absolutely determined to hang on. It took six hours for her body to finally drain and close down, and I held her the whole time.

It was five to one in the morning exactly. Something made me look down at her. She wasn't breathing . . . and . . . she wasn't breathing . . . and . . . she wasn't breathing. Piers was out of the room. I wasn't quite sure, but I didn't think she had died, although she wasn't breathing. I was muddled about what was happening. I sent Rebecca to get Piers. He came into the room, pale and close to tears. Something told me she wasn't quite dead. When Piers came in, it was almost as if she was waiting for her father to appear. She suddenly . . . breathed. And as she did that, the most fantastic thing happened – it's so true – something – her soul – left her, and then it was not Isobel. I knew then she was dead. She died with a smile on her face, looking up at me.

Suddenly, there seemed to be so many people in the room. I wished Piers and I had been left on our own, with no nurse, no doctor, no vicar, just us, so we could look at her and feel her. It was rather like having a baby – the first thing you do is tell people it's finally happened. Within what seemed like minutes to me, Mummy was over, my brother was over, we were all drinking brandy, and it was almost like a party. It was too quick. But when you're in that situation you don't really have any control. You're in such shock when it finally happens you just let things happen. People were only with us because they wanted to be a comfort.

A couple of days later I rang the faithhealer and told her; she was distraught, she thought she'd failed. I told her we would always be grateful. She'd given Isobel two weeks of happiness, two weeks she might never have had otherwise. She played an enormous part, and she gave Piers and me the strength to carry on. We always believed in her powers; what parent wouldn't try anything to comfort their dying child?

I didn't want Isobel to be touched by strangers. I didn't want her in a mortuary, so she stayed at home. I'd already decided what little dress she was going to wear. I really wanted to dress her myself. We were lucky we knew she was going to die so we had time to think about what we wanted. When an accident is the cause of death, the bereaved have very little time to plan details of this kind.

We carried Isobel's body upstairs to her room to wash and dress her. I noticed straight away that her night-light wasn't on. We always switched it on every evening when she went to bed, even when she was ill. I flicked it on and it didn't work. I thought the bulb must have gone, but I couldn't believe the timing. It must have gone out when Isobel was dying – it couldn't simply have been coincidence.

I so much wanted to wash and dress her but when I carried her upstairs, I felt it wasn't her. She was sunken; it just wasn't her, and I couldn't do it. I couldn't wash her hair. I left her with the nurse and Rebecca. I felt such a failure; I couldn't do this for my own daughter. I thought she'd be wondering if I was disgusted by her. I wasn't disgusted – I was frightened. This was the first time I'd ever seen anybody dead. I think it all became too much for me. I wish it hadn't. I had felt sure that nature would look after me at that point; after all it had carried me through the whole seven weeks. But not this time. I suppose nurturing her dead body would have done me more harm than good.

I asked Rebecca to cut a lock from Isobel's blonde hair so that I would have her first lock and her last. (I have them now in my bedroom, in little pots.) She was in her cot, and it was as though she was just lying there sleeping normally. I imagined her duvet moving. I suppose I was having illusions. The nurse put a nappy on her before lying her in the cot, which confused me. I'd never known that some bodily functions still happen even after death. Everything shuts down, and the last bit of life is expunged. That upset me again, because it represented another aspect of finality. Eventually we all went to bed. I thought I'd be able to stay in her bedroom, but I couldn't: it was so cold. She stayed in there until the funeral three days later.

After Isobel died, Emily was a totally different baby. During Isobel's last week she'd been deeply unhappy, crying a lot. My nerves were so stretched I couldn't stand her screaming. Despite it being mid-December, Rebecca took her out in her pram so it made it easier for us to cope with Isobel, and to give poor Emily a break and calm her down. But when Isobel died, she was back to her happy self. She obviously sensed the relief we were feeling because Isobel was no longer in pain. Thank goodness she was as young as she was. If she'd been a couple of months older she would have been so disturbed.

The next day the undertaker came to measure Isobel. He looked at her lying there and said how beautiful she was. A few days later the coffin arrived. I wasn't expecting it to be white and it made me think of an

angel. It was terribly difficult when the undertaker
came to put her in. She had a favourite teddy that
always went to bed with her at night. I thought teddy
would look after her. He asked me how I wanted her
laid, which I hadn't really thought about. I was shocked
by how squashed it was, how it was moulded to her
body. It was tiny and she absolutely rock hard.

I asked him to put teddy under her arm. I couldn't
bring myself to lift her arm. It was ice, ice cold, and the
coldness disturbed and hurt me more than anything.
She had one arm hugging teddy in the same way she
used to lie in her cot. He didn't nail the lid on, not until
the day of the funeral. Once she was in her coffin and
the lid was on I felt slightly calmer.

Piers found it very comforting to spend time in her
room. He felt that looking at her was his way of letting
the reality sink in. He kept on saying to himself, 'She's
dead,' really drumming it in. Over the days before the
funeral he did some very intense grieving, so intense it
frightened me.

I didn't want Isobel's body to frighten me. I wanted
to remember Isobel alive. I'd seen enough of her to
realise she was dead, but there was no way I could have
stayed in her room in the same way as Piers. When I
went to bed, Piers would go into Isobel's room and sit
there for hours. I felt guilty that he could and I
couldn't. I felt I was betraying Isobel in some way, but in
the end I realised that we were grieving in different
ways, and decided I wouldn't pressure myself to grieve
against my nature.

No one had ever told me what death was like. I wished
I'd known what happened. I wished I'd been taught
about the actual process of death, about what to expect.
When Isobel was dying on my lap and only had about a

week to live, I thought about how it would happen. I thought she would just die and there would be no confusion. But death through illness isn't like that. It's a very slow process, and a dying person goes through many different stages. Isobel nearly died six times that week. Yet the picture you get on television of people dying is one minute they're alive, the next they're dead. In my experience, death is not like that.

Isobel was gone. Suddenly there was absolutely nothing to do except organise the funeral. Piers and I had both been so busy and focused for two months, then there was nothing. That's when our problems really started. We were both tense, upset and mentally and physically exhausted. And suddenly we had nothing to keep ourselves occupied. I was angry and I started taking it out on Piers, the person who was closest to me. Before Isobel died, I had a toddler who demanded a lot of attention; my days were filled with doing things with Isobel. Then quite suddenly she was gone and I was left with dear Emily, who at that age just slept. I found it hard to adjust suddenly to a completely different way of life.

During those days when we were organising the funeral I started writing down all my feelings and emotions because I was so surprised at how intense they were. It was the first time I had a chance to look back and reflect, the first time I wondered how we had coped. I wondered how I could have gone through it. As her mother, I had to – she needed me. I did it for her. I gave every ounce of love I had to that child, and I was also trying to support Piers. I could not have prepared myself for the death of my child. I had to rely on an inner strength, an inner strength I'd never thought I possessed.

Chapter Six

I wanted the funeral to be very special for Isobel, something she would have liked, especially as it was her birthday. I didn't want boring hymns, so I gave a tape of Isobel's favourite nursery rhymes and songs to the organ player – all the tunes that she could identify with – and they were played as people walked into the church. She had 'Puff the Magic Dragon' and 'All Things Bright and Beautiful'. I chose 'Abide With Me' for myself – it's such a beautiful hymn, and I was sure Isobel wouldn't mind.

I purposely wore black. People might have thought it was too sombre, but wearing black illustrated how I was feeling, and I didn't care what other people thought. I wanted to wear black out of respect, not only to her funeral, but for a couple of days. I would have been one of those people in the old days who felt right wearing black for a whole year. I saw it as a personal symbol, recognising the fact that I was grieving, but also a way of signifying to others that I was in mourning. I wanted to mourn for Isobel and I wanted it to be known that I was mourning. I knew Isobel would have wanted me to do as I felt best. I didn't want people saying to me that I should be celebrating what life she had because she'd only had two years.

I was advised by my mother and Dr Boodle to take a

very small dose of valium before the funeral, because I didn't want to be hysterical and miss everything. I wanted to relish her funeral, to really listen, appreciate and soak up the atmosphere. I wanted to remember my daughter's funeral. And I wanted the valium just to take the edge off, without doping me or making me glassy-eyed. I wanted to sit and listen to the vicar's address, and for it to be bearable for a couple of hours. I didn't want to take any chances.

I tied a little silver helium balloon on to Isobel's coffin. She would have wanted that. They were all around her cot in Great Ormond Street Hospital, and she loved them. I wanted to cut the balloon before she was buried so that it would go up to her. I didn't care what people thought of this.

On the way to the chapel, I looked and saw the flowers on her coffin and I said to Piers, 'This shouldn't be happening.' It felt like a clip from a classic film. And when I saw the way her coffin was carried into the church, I was dumbstruck. I'd expected it to be carried in the traditional way by four people. Because she was only a child, the undertaker carried her like a baby. That was sad. We walked down the aisle and I just couldn't believe the way he was carrying her. The helium balloon kept catching the light and it just wafted in the breeze. It would have been her second birthday.

People asked me if I was going to take Emily to the church. Of course she came – Isobel was her sister! I took great pride in dressing Emily. Rebecca had given her a sweet little outfit which was meant to be for Christmas, and she wore that to the funeral. It was a special occasion, and I wanted Emily to look smart. I could quite easily not have cared, but I'm so glad I did. During a quiet moment in the funeral service Emily wailed, just once, as if she was saying her own goodbye to Isobel in her own baby way. Lots of people remarked on it afterwards. In the end, I only really cried once, during 'Abide With Me'. It's such a beautiful hymn and it reminded me that Isobel had been such a beautiful little girl.

Piers and I wanted the vicar to tell everybody how brave Isobel had been in hospital, what she'd been like as a little girl, how she'd loved animals, and that she was a happy, contented child with an air that just drew people to her. We wanted him to tell everyone how, just thirty-six hours after her operation, she'd stood up and walked with a happy smiling face. After the address we asked the vicar to read the most beautiful poem, called 'God's Lent Child'. It meant a lot to us, and has given us an awful lot of comfort. I had it written and framed, and it now hangs in our bedroom.

God's Lent Child

I'll lend you for a little while a child of mine, God said,
For you to love the while she lives, and mourn for when she's dead.
It may be six or seven years, or forty-two or three,
But will you, 'til I call her back, take care of her for me?
She'll bring her charms to gladden you. And should her stay be brief,
You'll always have your memories as solace in your grief.
I cannot promise she will stay, since all from earth return,
But there are lessons taught below I want this child to learn.
I've looked this whole world over in my search for

teachers true,
And from the folk that crowd Life's lane I have
    chosen you.
Now will you give her all your love and not think
    the labour vain,
Nor hate me when I come to take this lent child
    back again?
I fancy that I heard them say, 'Dear God, Thy will
    be done.
For all the joys this child will bring the risk of grief
    we'll run.
We will shelter her with tenderness, we'll love her
    while we may,
And for all the happiness we've ever known, we'll
    ever grateful stay,
But should the angels call her much sooner than
    we'd planned,
We will brave the bitter grief that comes, and try to
    understand.

Anon.

We went to bury her and it all happened too quickly.
The ribbon was cut, the balloon went up, she was in the
ground before I knew it. All I wanted, oh God I wish, all
I wanted was to stand by her grave and look at her
coffin, look at her for the very last time. Yet I felt I had
to pull myself away, because everyone else wanted to
pay their last respects. I felt under pressure at my
own daughter's funeral. Instead of concentrating on
her I was worrying about everyone else. I so desperately
wanted just to be alone with Piers by her graveside and
for everyone else to pay their respects at another time.
We lost that personal goodbye.

People say it's helpful to invite people back to your
home after a funeral, but all I wanted was to be by

myself. What do you say to people? What do they say to you? Yet it's a tradition, with everyone offering you support. The truth is, you don't need it so much there and then over a cup of coffee, you need it much more afterwards in the days, weeks, months and even years to follow.

Some people close to me assumed that it was better for me to cope by not talking about my loss. They wanted to see me back to normal, back to the sunny person I used to be. No sooner had Isobel been buried than people who had meant the most to her started to back off. They wanted to block out her death because it was so horrific. People wanted Piers and me to be the people we were before, to act normally. They didn't like to see emotion, to see how grief-stricken, how awful we were feeling. They preferred that we put on a brave front and pretend nothing had happened, because they couldn't cope with it. Those who thought it would help us by pretending everything was okay were in fact doing the worst possible thing. I wanted them to listen, not run away, just listen. That was all – they didn't have to say anything, just stick by me and listen.

Not saying anything was the cruellest response, even if it was intended not to offend, but saying the wrong thing was also hurtful. People said, 'At least you have your husband.' In fact they couldn't have been more wrong. The death of a child puts an enormous amount of strain on a marriage. Piers loved Isobel, she was his life, but he didn't want to bring her up in conversation; and all I wanted to do was talk about her. He would say, 'She's dead, she isn't here any more, you've got to concentrate on Emily. You've got to make the effort to put Isobel aside.' But I didn't see it like that. I let nature take care of me. I decided to grieve in the way my body and mind were telling me to grieve. There was constant pressure from other people, telling me what to do and what not to do. The last thing I needed was to be made to feel guilty for not wanting to do something.

There were times when I could have packed my suitcase and walked away. I don't think I would ever have left Piers for good, but at the time, it felt much better not being with him. I thought that if he couldn't give me the sympathy and support I needed, who else could I get it from, but Isobel? At times like that, life was not worth living. All we seemed to be doing was shouting at each other. Our lives had completely changed. We took a giant leap into a world which was going to be very, very different. I'd always thought that when someone died, it was tragic, you felt sad – but you got over it. I couldn't have been more wrong.

Chapter Seven

The day after the funeral I found myself packing Emily's suitcase. My family happened to be spending Christmas abroad, and they had booked tickets for Piers and me to go with them. We thought it would be good for us to have a break, so my mother-in-law looked after Emily. Up until that point, I'd hardly thought of dear Emily, and she could sense, even at such a tender age, that things weren't right. When I found myself packing her suitcase I felt awful, because I didn't want to see Emily go. I wanted to put everything into Emily, but I was shoving her away, and it didn't make sense. Piers really wanted to go abroad, to escape the house where Isobel had died. I felt a lot of unease about going, but we both needed the rest.

I hated seeing Emily go – it tore my heart. The day before we were due to fly out, the house was totally empty with both our children gone. I didn't even have Emily to hug. I wish now that she'd come with us.

On holiday I was surrounded by loving family, but it proved to be a disaster, because they seemed to find it difficult to mention Isobel. For seven weeks I'd done everything I could for her; suddenly she wasn't there, and now I was expected to lie there and read books as if nothing had happened. One book I did find helpful, however, was called *On the Death of a Child* by John G.

Williams, whose own daughter died at the age of eight. It helped me to begin to seek a spiritual understanding of Isobel's death, but I still had a lot of grieving ahead of me. More than anything I needed to talk, and no one talked. I have never felt more alone. Even on Christmas Day people wished me Happy Christmas, which I found absurd. I couldn't face going to church. My own daughter had not celebrated her second birthday, so how could I celebrate the birth of Jesus?

I wanted to talk about Isobel but Piers didn't. The rows started because we were coping in totally different ways. At one point when I was terribly distraught, instead of giving me a hug he shook me, telling me once more that Isobel was dead and I was never going to see her again. I didn't want to hear it again – I didn't need to hear it at all. I just wanted a quiet talk and reassuring hug, but he was in such torture as well. All we could do was clash with each other.

Exactly a week after the funeral we were lying by the pool when my mother noticed a solitary, plain, silver helium balloon floating across the garden, just like the one I'd tied on to Isobel's coffin. I was always looking for a sign, always thinking, 'I hope she's okay.' And that was my sign. I was terribly comforted by that; it gave me reassurance.

I had another sign the night before we left to go home. I was very aware of what I was going back to. I was feeling very tired, sad, emotional, and I decided to go for a walk along the beach by myself. It was about five o'clock in the evening, so the beach was fairly empty. I walked the full stretch, came back again, thought I'd had enough, and started walking towards the house. But just as I was getting to the gate, I changed my mind. I didn't feel quite ready to go back to face everybody, so I walked a bit more.

I did exactly the same thing, up and down the beach, the whole time thinking about Isobel. I was going over and over the same thoughts, wondering what it was like up there, what form Isobel had taken, how old she was, if she was still a child or an adult, if she could see me – all these questions. Above all I was hoping that she wasn't too homesick for me. When you've looked after a child for two years, you panic when you leave it with a new babysitter for a couple of hours. It was the same feeling of suddenly not having your child with you, of being parted from someone you gave life to. My natural, maternal response was to wonder constantly if Isobel was all right.

I had tears streaming down my face, when suddenly something made me lift my head. That's when I noticed another single, silver helium balloon. I had no idea where it came from. It was about ten feet away from me, quite low, almost at head height – maybe a bit above. I think it had been waiting for me to come back up to that point of the beach to let itself go, because unlike helium balloons that usually travel straight up, this one floated horizontally in front of my eyes. It was extraordinary. The moment I saw this balloon, I didn't have to wonder, I knew Isobel was guiding it. It was just as if she was replying to my thoughts. I watched the balloon waft straight past me, straight out to sea, horizontally; the further it went away from me, the more it began to rise. It was an unbelievable sign.

After what proved in the end to be an unhelpful holiday for Piers and me, the thought of having to go back together to an empty house was very difficult. When we walked through the front door, the silence was awful. Suddenly reality hit us. It was all very well to fantasise on a beach, but when we returned home, it was the real thing. Half of me wanted to escape and the other half wanted to sit quietly and talk about Isobel and how we were both feeling.

Until the day Isobel died, everybody had been so supportive, always asking if there was anything they could do, how I was coping and feeling. When we returned from holiday the contrast was staggering. There was such an air of finality. It was all too horrific for anybody to talk about. Meanwhile, Piers and I were snapping at each other. I didn't want to be with him. We were trying desperately to cope with our own emotions, and didn't have enough room to take on the other person's way of coping. He not only got my anger, but also the last thing he wanted to hear – my feelings about Isobel. I so wanted to talk to him, but all he would say was, 'You're repeating yourself, I've heard it all before, stop it, you're boring – Isobel's dead!' He would end up cutting me off.

As the first couple of weeks went by, Piers wanted to shut it out and pretend to everybody he was okay, that everything was back to normal, and he didn't want to have me as the reminder. I was desperate to talk, I couldn't talk about anything else. Nothing else mattered, and I didn't want to let Isobel go. In the end, my response was to cut Piers off. He'd want to hug me but I didn't want to be hugged by someone who wouldn't let me talk. I thought he was being hypocritical, so my response was to freeze him out.

Piers refused to let anything get in the way of his normal life. So if we were invited to a dinner party he would think nothing of it and reason that it would do me good, whereas I would have to say: 'I'm sorry, I can't do it.' Sometimes he was fine and he'd understand; other times he'd say, 'Oh come on, you've got to do it at some point.' He was telling me how to grieve. I'd say to him, 'You can do it, I can't. Why can't we leave it at that. We should respect how each other is coping.'

One evening, I made an effort to go out with Piers and try to enjoy ourselves together. It was a friend's dinner party, and I was sitting next to a man I'd never met before. He knew about Isobel's death, and seemed charming. We started discussing his interest in astronomy. He told me he didn't believe in heaven, and that when someone died, that was it: nothing. People should forget and look forwards, he said. It was as if an electric shock had passed through my body. I told him how Isobel's nightlight had died at exactly the same time as she did, and that I supposed he thought that was a coincidence. He said of course it was. I was on the verge of breaking down. He then said he didn't think it was the time or place to have this conversation. I asked him why not, couldn't he cope? He replied by saying he didn't know me well enough. I left that table as fast as I could. His insensitivity and lack of tact – words simply failed me.

In those first weeks we were too traumatised to think rationally. We had to have someone in the middle as a mediator, to explain why we were behaving like we were and that it was perfectly normal. I don't know what I would have done without Jennie, our liaison sister from Great Ormond Street Hospital. She was amazing. She never said a wrong word, she was always there when I needed help. She had no training, just experience in dealing with bereaved parents. She would point out to each of us why we were thinking a certain thing of the other, and in the end we came to a far deeper understanding of each other.

I also started seeing a psychotherapist. All she knew was that Isobel had died, so I started from the very beginning. I described my mind as a ball of wool in complete tangle, and her job was to unravel it. Quite often when I visited her I thought I'd have nothing to say, but somehow when I got there, there was always something. Such an enormous trauma brought up all sorts of things I hadn't thought about for years.

I decided to keep Rebecca on after Isobel's death to help with Emily. I was under a great deal of stress and felt I needed to be able to get out of the house whenever I wanted. I also thought that the more time I grieved for Isobel the more time I would have later on for Emily. I wanted to be a good mother to Emily, and if that meant she had to wait for me to grieve properly for Isobel, then that was the way it had to be.

Emily was meant to be christened in November, the month before Isobel died. We postponed it until April because even I thought I'd feel better by then and would be able to cope with it. But by February I realised I how wrong I'd been. I knew then it was too soon; I couldn't have gone through with it. The reality of having lost my daughter was only just setting in. Grieving was taking a huge amount of time, and I wasn't prepared to rush it. On the other hand Piers wanted to pretend everything was all right; he would go through any amount of pain to prove to people that he was okay. Meanwhile, I was too heartbroken to deal with the social side of a christening. So I reasoned with Piers that in view of all this it would either be best if we postponed Emily's christening for a second time, or to do it very quietly at home with just the vicar.

I told him I couldn't go through with it, it would be too painful, that I was sure Emily wouldn't mind; she was too young to understand anyway. I didn't want to stand in the church where Isobel's funeral had been, having a ceremony. I didn't want to be in any church. I

honestly believed Piers would understand, that he'd
agree and we'd postpone it for another couple of
months. I didn't think I was asking too much. To my
surprise, he felt quite the opposite and told me that we
had to go ahead with it because otherwise we'd put
everybody out again. He was thinking of everybody
else and not how I was feeling. I thought people would
understand. In the end we did not have Emily's christening until she was thirteen months old, and we had it
at home instead of in church.

As Emily was still quite young, I had a lot of time to
myself to think. We always made a point of leaving Isobel's bedroom door open. I went into Isobel's room a
couple of times, but it didn't make me feel any better. It
was very hard, so I stopped doing it. It was enough for
me to be able to see her cupboard with the door open,
and to see her little nightlight and possessions on top
of the cupboard. That was all the reminding I could
handle.

One evening I put Emily to bed and I was drawn into
Isobel's room. I don't know why I decided to go in. It
was a spur of the moment decision. I hadn't been in
there for three weeks or more. It was quiet. I sat in her
rocking chair and looked into her cot. What was usually
a rather empty, cold room, suddenly became full of
warmth, full of Isobel. I wasn't consciously aware of Isobel being there, I just felt warm inside, comfortable,
and reassured. It was just like being in Isobel's room
when she was alive. I felt really peaceful and at ease with
life. I must have sat there for five or more minutes. I got
up, touched her cot and walked out. I remember thinking to myself that it felt so comforting I would do it
again the following evening.

The next day I went into Isobel's room, sat down in

her rocking chair – and burst out crying. She wasn't
there. I think it was then I realised that perhaps she'd
been in the room the day before. The difference was
unbelievable. It was back to the cold, empty room that
hadn't been helpful. It was extraordinary. I couldn't
have imagined the difference in feeling, in temperature, in atmosphere. I really believe it was Isobel's way
of saying, 'Mummy, I'm all right, I'm with you.'

SPRING 1992

Chapter Eight

For the first couple of months after Isobel's death, although my every thought was about her, I was hyperactive. It was a form of escapism to fill my days. Sometimes I invited friends to supper just to fill the house with noise. During the day I couldn't just sit in the house. The silence was too dreadful, and the pain that came in waves, too intense, too agonising. It came in sharp stabbing jabs. In between the jabs there was a shocked numbness. I often felt as though I was spinning around the room – all I could do was keep moving in small circles. I felt completely helpless. The feelings I experienced in the first six weeks were so varied and so intense they frightened me. I felt a lot of anger and it was mostly directed at God. I kept asking why, why us, why Isobel? That's when I first started looking for a book that might help give me some answers to my questions.

I had been so looking forward to Isobel starting school and found it difficult to drive past what would have been her school. I didn't even want to see her little friends. I missed that girl more than anyone could describe. The feeling of pain was almost too much to bear. There was nothing I could take for it – I just had to go through it. I never knew there could be pain like it.

People would say to me, 'You'll get over it.' But I felt I never would. I decided I wouldn't tidy out Isobel's room. I didn't want to put her away just yet. Most days I waited for Piers to come home from work so I could talk to him about Isobel and how I was feeling, but I had to put up with him not wanting to talk. There was still tremendous friction in our marriage as a result.

Three months after Isobel's death, reality really started setting in. I felt as though I had a broken heart. I couldn't enjoy spring, I was yearning for Isobel too much. As the seasons changed, they highlighted the fact that Isobel was no longer around. I couldn't forget, because I was constantly being reminded of her absence. I desperately wanted to cuddle her, and hear her voice and little feet running down the passage again. It was my birthday at the end of March, but I didn't feel like celebrating; how could I have a happy birthday? I tried hard to put my heart into conversations but I found it so difficult. I was so dazed, and no one seemed to understand, no one could guess how I was really feeling. Acting a part became all too familiar to me.

All I wanted was for people to accept the fact that I was miserable, not to pretend that nothing had happened. I couldn't understand why death wasn't discussed freely by everybody in society, instead of being left to church leaders, obituary writers, coroners and the bereaved. I couldn't understand why people seemed to be embarrassed by talking about death; after all, it happens to us all. But after three or four months, I was expected to behave as if nothing had happened. How could I, when the pain I was feeling was so physical? My heart actually hurt, my chest hurt. It was a very deep, intense ache, and became even more acute when I looked at a picture of Isobel or when someone reminded me of her. It would hit a nerve. When I cried for her the pain was even deeper, but at the same time I could feel the pain being relieved through crying. In a funny way it was exquisite pain. I could actually feel it so much that it was nice – I was getting such a vivid picture of her.

There were times when I wanted to escape that pain, but I had to go through it, I had to grieve. At the same time I had to give my body a break from the intensity and I became very restless. This restlessness and hyper-activity continued for months. I just couldn't stop; it was my way of coping. Instead of hiding away from every-body I did the exact opposite. I couldn't talk to Piers, so I brought people into the house. Two months after Iso-bel died I was giving dinner parties. It didn't mean I didn't think of Isobel, it just made it easier at that par-ticular point in my grief. It was so intense that the only way my mind and body could cope with it was by break-ing it up and camouflaging it. Yet if anyone asked how I was, I would tell them and start talking about Isobel.

I felt much better on home ground where I was boss, and where I could relax. I didn't set out to have a rou-tine, the routine found me. After three or four months, I found it helped if I set myself some kind of goal each day – this was progress. In the early days I couldn't have managed that. Just getting through each day was an effort. The house was suddenly difficult to keep tidy, any mundane chore was terribly difficult. Some morn-ings it was even difficult to get out of bed. I felt I had nothing to get up for. What helped me get out of this rut was reviving my interest in horses. I found they really helped me. I was lucky enough to have a friend called Debbie, who said, 'Come on, I'm going to get you up on a horse again. Let's go for a hack and see if you like it.' If she'd pressured me I wouldn't have wanted to, but she knew just how far to push me.

I did learn to ride again. It was a tremendous challenge and terribly therapeutic, because I had to concentrate for that half an hour a couple of times a week. That was the only time my brain had a rest from Isobel, when I had no option but to listen to Debbie's instructions. There was no way I could think about Isobel during the lessons. It gave my whole body and mind a valuable half-hour break. Otherwise I was thinking about Isobel twenty-four hours a day, and being tuned into the one thing day in, day out was exhausting. Through riding, I kept busy. I enjoyed it and it gave me a kickstart.

I was still having downs I never thought I would recover from. I couldn't think straight, and continued to experience such frighteningly mixed emotions I thought I was going mad. On one occasion I actually put the sellotape in the fridge, although I couldn't remember doing it. My memory and concentration were appalling, and quite often I stopped talking in mid-sentence, unable to remember what I was talking about. On my better days I was able to think more rationally. I thought of all the positive things that might come out of Isobel's death, like learning to be a bereavement counsellor and helping other people. But during the desperate days of pain and anguish, when all I really felt like giving up, it was very hard to think positively. There were times when all I could do was just sit in a heap on the floor and say over and over: 'When is this going to end, I can't manage, please let me rest.' Then the numbness would return, giving me weeks sometimes when I wouldn't be able to feel a thing, not one single emotion, nothing. Talking to me was like talking to a brick wall. When I thought of Isobel I felt nothing. I realised nature was protecting me from the pain by making me numb.

Some months later, the initial numbness of the shock wore off and reality set in; the pain was so great I couldn't cope. I felt very lonely and isolated, and felt that nobody except a few people understood how I felt. I thought of going to bereavement support groups, but I didn't want to face complete strangers who were all at different stages of grieving. I didn't want to mix my grief with theirs, or put myself into a group with special needs which was in a way separated from society. I wanted society to come to me. I wanted people to accept and try to understand how I was feeling and not run away from it. I needed every bit of one-to-one support I could get to help me through such extraordinary feelings that were completely different from one hour to the next.

All I wanted was to be with Isobel. One day I was ironing. I was on my own, feeling isolated, distraught because I felt that no one understood how low I was feeling. Piers was coping in his own way; I couldn't support him and he couldn't support me, and I felt dreadfully lonely. If someone had come in at that moment and said something like, 'Don't worry, you'll feel better soon,' or 'Come on, get to grips,' I was feeling so imbalanced I honestly would not have trusted my reaction. I didn't think of anybody – my only focus was Isobel. I missed her so desperately that life held nothing for me at that precise moment. Then, suddenly I had the extraordinary feeling that she was in the room; I thought Isobel was saying to me, 'Come to me.' I could almost feel the pull of her presence.

Looking back, I'm sure she wasn't saying 'Come to me'; I'm sure she was saying, 'I'm here, you're going to be all right, I'm with you,' but because I was so grief-stricken, because I couldn't think logically, all I felt at that moment was Isobel pulling me to her, one way and one way only. It was like tunnel vision. I didn't see what was on either side at all, I was feeling so desperate for her that nothing else mattered: not even my life.

I had a mental picture of how I saw myself. I imagined a line; above the line I was okay – that was light. Underneath was a mass of dark cloud. I saw myself as on the borderline, on the verge of going into that big dark cloud. If I hadn't been advised to take anti-depressants I don't know what I would have done. I would be driving along in the car, and I'd start thinking about how I was going to end my life. Maybe I'd just veer towards the other side of the road and into an oncoming car? The fact that I was even thinking about it was a terrifying realisation. If I hadn't told my doctor my life would have been in danger. Jennie from Great Ormond Street and our vicar and his wife were also very supportive. But I still couldn't talk to any of my family, because I felt they didn't know what to say or how to cope. Knowing that I was thinking about taking my own life would have been too much for them to take on.

During this period, it helped me to try and do things for myself and no one else. I started having aromatherapy every now and then. It didn't camouflage my hurt or help me to escape it in any way, but it did help my body get through a terribly stressful time. I also felt that it was helping my mind. A massage didn't make the pain go away, but I felt it was good for my body, so in that way I helped myself physically, and hoped it might rub off mentally.

I became very aware of the power I had to really let my appearance go. It was extraordinary that I never did. In fact, I refused to. I thought if I let myself go physically that would have been the last straw. I would have just faded away. Going to the gym every day and learning to ride again after fifteen years really helped me physically, and gave me the strength to carry on. It gave me a little bit of self-respect to hang on to.

In the end, I went to the opposite extreme. I was obsessed with getting out of the house and working out at the gym. It was a way of channelling my anger through the exercise machines. My anger was going somewhere, instead of being directed at Piers. I felt I had a positive glow. If anything I became hooked on exercise because it made me feel good, and I hadn't thought that was possible. I went through various different hairstyles in one year. What I was trying to do was find myself. I was a changed person, and the way I saw myself in the mirror had to catch up with who I really was.

Our marriage was still under a great deal of strain; we were snapping at each other and not communicating. So we decided to take a holiday in Greece to spend some time alone together. It was our first summer without Isobel, and I was dreading the holiday. I saw it was a make-or-break situation, and expected us to be at loggerheads. It would just be the two of us for two whole weeks. I was even nervous about whether we'd have anything to talk about.

By the time we arrived, Piers was already beginning to relax, and to think more sensitively. Within a couple of days, he started to listen to me, to appreciate what was going on in my mind. Away from work, he was doing his upmost to make me feel more comfortable, and because I felt more comfortable with his approach, I was more relaxed. It was the first time he didn't tense up when I raised the subject of Isobel; it was as if a valve had been opened, and he was now willing to share a little of what was going on in his own mind.

Piers became far more open than he had been in the six months since Isobel had died, and he wasn't ashamed to show his tears. Up until then he'd been crying in private. Now he was openly grieving, and that really made a difference. He volunteered information about how he was feeling. One morning he woke up very sullen and quiet. Over breakfast I asked him what was wrong, and instead of saying, 'Nothing,' as usual, he told me he'd had an awful dream about Isobel and started crying. I was so relieved to see that he could grieve openly. That was such a comfort for me, and I think it did him a lot of good. He was actually being himself; I could see the Piers I had married, not the stranger who could cut me off and not share his feelings.

I realised for the first time in months that I really did love Piers; I actually felt my love for him returning. Until then I hadn't known what I felt for him. I wasn't going to say I loved him as things had been. I'd also been putting so much love into Isobel and then, when Isobel died, concentrating on my love for Emily, that there wasn't enough room for Piers. All I could do was hope that we would survive. That holiday I found myself saying to Piers that I loved him very much, and that I thought we'd be okay after all. That was the turning point for both of us, the point when we started getting to know each other again.

WINTER 1992

Chapter Nine

It was in October, almost to the day that Isobel had been diagnosed, that I started to notice Emily was twitching on one side of her face. Every time she turned around her left eye would close. I put it down to her eye condition, ptosis. I didn't worry too much until the twitches turned into what looked like spasms. Her eye closed completely, especially in bright light, and her cheek creased up. I took her to a paediatric eye specialist who advised us that she should have an MRI brain scan as a precautionary measure.

As soon as I heard 'MRI', I went into shock. It was exactly what Isobel had gone through. My whole body went numb, I could feel the blood drain from my face. The eye specialist knew about Isobel, and tried to reassure me. He didn't let us know at the time, but he was extremely worried that Emily's condition was connected to Isobel's, and immediately informed Great Ormond Street.

This time I took Emily to a private hospital so she could have the brain scan as soon as possible, and because there was no way I could have gone back to Great Ormond Street – the memories would have been impossible to bear. She was booked in for four days' time. I drove home, dead calm, surprisingly level-headed, and rang Piers at the office to tell him. He was shattered. We spent the next four days fearing the worst. It was only natural. It seemed to us that history was repeating itself. On the day of her scan, I had to hold Emily while she was being gassed, and it was just like watching Isobel going under. Once again, somehow we got through it. We were both amazingly calm and supportive of each other. Although both of us were extremely tense, we weren't snapping at each other. Nothing really fazed us, we'd been through it all before. And I was sure God wouldn't take Emily away from us – he just wouldn't.

Emily had the scan in the afternoon, and we had the results through that evening. Her brain was absolutely clear, and the twitching apparently a mannerism. Although her symptoms suggested that there might be a problem in her brain stem, the brain scan happily proved otherwise, and a possible genetic link with Isobel's tumour was also disproved. I'm sure it was a lesson from God. I'd had to push thoughts of Isobel to the back of my mind, and to think of the possibility of Emily either being seriously ill or dying. I realised I was very lucky to have Emily. Before then Isobel had always been at the forefront of my mind, and Emily was just there. I felt that it was God's way of showing us how lucky we were to have her.

As the anniversary of Isobel's death approached, I could remember her so vividly, but in fleeting images. I could see her face, but only one expression, hovering in front of my eyes, and then she would disappear. I dreaded the long, dark evenings, because I associated them with Isobel's illness.

Half of me was looking forward to Christmas; the other half was thinking of Isobel. When I thought of what a fantastic family Christmas we could have had I felt so angry. Isobel would have been three. She would have understood about Christmas for the first time. When I went shopping and saw all those happy people buying presents for the festive season, looking as if they didn't have a care in the world, I felt so envious. I couldn't help but look at them and think how happy they looked compared to me. My morbid thoughts at Christmas time seemed so inappropriate. In the end I decided Isobel would want me to make Christmas special for Emily, so I threw myself into it. I thought to myself, 'Isobel's having a wonderful time up there, so I'm going to do the same for Emily.'

I lived in dread of the anniversary, so much so I think I did all my really hard grieving the month before. When the time actually came, the pain wasn't as bad as I had expected. I'd reached the stage where I knew it would have been fantastic if Isobel was alive, but she wasn't; there was no way I could bring her back, and I had to face up to that.

We planned the anniversary very badly. She died in the early hours of 16 December. Piers decided to take the day off on the 16th, but if we'd thought about it a little more clearly what he should have done was take the day off on the 15th, the day leading up to her death. When I put Emily to bed on the Tuesday, the 15th, Piers was still at work. Isobel had started dying at 7.45 that evening, exactly a year before. I was suddenly alone.

Fortunately Piers arrived very shortly afterwards. I was distraught, because I hadn't prepared for the memories being so vivid. I was literally reliving her death. It was agony for about an hour. I was frightened because the feelings were so strong; I was clock-watching, imagining her draining, holding her. I could even remember the little flicker of her eyelashes, I could feel her hand wasting because she hadn't eaten; I remembered it so clearly it was almost as though her hand was in mine. It felt so thin, so soft, as if her bones were no longer hard. I remembered those details absolutely, as if they were under a microscope; it was very unnerving.

I had a few glasses of wine, which eased the pain and I went to bed early. Emily woke up at about 3.30am; as soon as I realised what time it was I felt a huge wave of relief wash over me, because I knew Isobel had died by now and was no longer in pain.

Isobel's headstone had only just been put on her grave a week before the anniversary of her death and I thought it would be special if it was blessed on 19 December – her birthday. We went to the florist and bought a silver helium balloon, exactly the same as the one she had a year before. I bought another one with a teddy bear on it for Emily and tied it onto her pushchair. Then we walked up to her grave, where we met the vicar and my family. It was cold, damp, depressing. He gave a short blessing and we tied the balloon onto her grave. When I saw her name in writing, the dates, the words, it was very difficult, and so painful. She would have been three, oozing with health, and playing with Emily. It was very, very hard. Tears streaked my face but I didn't care. Piers and I actually cried together. For the first time we were grieving for Isobel as a couple.

On Christmas Eve I decided to go to church, the first time I'd been since Isobel's death. It was a special service for children, and the church was absolutely packed. I sat at the back with Emily, and it was the first time I actually felt comfortable in a church since Isobel's death, as if I was meant to be there. I felt quite proud of myself; I actually quite enjoyed it. It was so warm and cosy; I'd never experienced that feeling of warmth before in a church and I was very moved by the service. That evening I sat down to wrap presents, which was awfully difficult. I gave Piers and Emily a stocking each. Rebecca had given Isobel a beautiful knitted stocking for her first Christmas, and I used that for Emily. I remember wrapping the presents, counting them and thinking that there should have been one more stocking, one more pile under the tree.

On Christmas Day we all went to church together. It was a really joyous occasion. I'm sure that Isobel was there in spirit. I could feel something I'd never felt before – this torch, this warmth, this glow. I felt as if I was one of God's special people, that he was somehow guiding me; that whatever bad things might happen there had to be a purpose behind them, and some good would come out of them. After dreading Christmas for so long, the three of us managed to sail through, and actually found pleasure in it, even though Isobel was gone.

A couple of days after Christmas I was feeling low again. I was overtired, sensitive – and pregnant, although I didn't know it yet. We had been staying with my in-laws, and one of the other guests made a comment about doing something with her two daughters. I just couldn't hold back my tears – it made me realise what Emily was missing out on – and I went to bed feeling more upset than ever. I had problems sleeping, until I finally dozed off and dreamed about Isobel. In my dream she was lying horizontal, her body was rock hard, dead, colourless, grey, just as I remember her in her coffin. Yet her face was alive; it had colour and life. In my dream I communicated with Isobel. She was saying to me: 'Mum, look at me, you can see. Here are my arms, they're dead and hard, my legs are the same, my tummy's the same. Now look at my face.' It was full of expression, just like that expression before she died.

She looked awfully peaceful but she was still alive. In those very intense few moments she was actually communicating with me. She was telling me that her body was dead, but *she* wasn't. Her face was saying: 'I'm still alive, my spirit is alive. I can see you and I'm with you all the time, don't worry.'

Then she began to die; she died again, and I watched her. She started to drain – it was so vivid. I woke up next morning feeling comforted and peaceful; everything was crystal clear. I was no longer upset. It was as if she'd visited me in my sleep. Although having watched her die again in my dream, which was so sad, it made me realise even more that her body was just a shell, that she was still very much alive in a different sense. I couldn't have imagined that scene. I long to see her again; I know it won't happen if I will it to, but only when I least expect it.

I decided after putting so much of myself into Isobel when she was alive that I should try and do the same for her after she died. It took a year for most of the anger and all of the numbness to fade; then all I could think about was finding a way of making up for her death, of creating something positive out of the loss of my child. So I tried to give Isobel a future. In my mind she's gone to a very special place. I can't help but wonder why she was taken; she was so lovely, so beautiful, she'd done no wrong. She didn't know the difference between right and wrong. The only way I can cope is to believe that she's gone somewhere much more beautiful, and that she will be with us as a family forever.

SPRING 1993

Chapter Ten

The peace didn't come for a very long time. It's only really just coming now, as I finish working on this book. I never stop missing Isobel, but as Emily grows older I'm gradually coming to terms with moving Isobel's things, and using them again. I've put Isobel's rocking chair in Emily's room, and Emily is wearing Isobel's pyjamas. I decided there was no point in buying a new pair, so, slowly, her room is being changed. It's still very difficult to open the cupboard and see the ankle boots she wore to help her walk; they bring back such painful memories.

I don't want people to think I'm putting Isobel on a pedestal. Naturally I realise she had her faults, but it's important to me that Isobel is remembered as a person, not just as someone who died painfully and tragically. I worry sometimes that I don't feel the same sort of love for Emily as I did for Isobel; but you always love your children differently; and I think this is highlighted when one of them is so very ill. When Isobel was dying, nature made me turn away from Emily and concentrate on Isobel. I would come back from Great Ormond Street Hospital too exhausted to feed her. All I could manage was a hug. I had very little left to give. Sometimes I felt guilty; sometimes other people made me feel guilty for being a bad and neglectful mother. But I came to realise that such mixed feelings were perfectly natural and understandable, and didn't mean that I didn't love Emily.

Emily is of course very special in her own right. She's like a first child reborn. She's so lucky to have known Isobel even for a short while; none of my other children will have that knowledge. I want her to know what happened, and for her to understand. She is a great comfort to me now and I feel very close to her. It's almost as if she knows how I'm feeling and wants to give me that extra hug to comfort me. I often talk about Isobel to her, and I always will, so that she'll grow up knowing that she had an elder sister. I feel I have to be honest. If she is wearing one of Isobel's cardigans for the first time, I tell her. I tell her if she's reading one of Isobel's books. When she walks downstairs, quite often she'll blow a little kiss in the direction of Isobel's picture, which hangs on the wall above.

No one will ever know the pain I feel, and that is so frustrating because I very much want to share it. Yesterday I lay in bed thinking that I had no one to talk to. All I could think of was how much I wanted to hug Isobel, and that's one thing I will never be able to do again. I don't feel whole, because part of me died with Isobel. I still have downs, which can hit me at any time. When I'm on a down, I have a constant, ongoing battle with myself, which is exhausting. Yet I can see my way out more clearly than I could a year ago, purely through the passage of time. I feel I must let myself come out of these times, that I shouldn't force my way out. Ignoring the down is refusing to grieve. People say to you, 'Oh, don't get depressed, try not to . . .' All I can say is, 'But I have to and there's nothing wrong with that – it's all part of grieving.'

I still find it very difficult seeing people I knew before Isobel's death. I'm sure they think I'm being anti-social. I don't want to lose them as friends; I hope they understand how traumatic it can be just seeing them. Their lives have all carried on; their children are growing up, and for me that hasn't happened. When I see my friends who still have two children, it highlights the fact that Isobel is no longer with us. It's too painful to watch them with their three-year-old when Isobel would have been the same age if she'd lived. Maybe in time I will get over that particular hurdle. Until then, I want to meet people Emily can meet for the first time, on her own terms. I hope people understand. Because I feel I've changed so much I want to wipe the slate clean, start afresh and meet people who don't remind me of Isobel. It doesn't mean I'm trying to forget Isobel: I just don't want to be reminded of what I've lost.

Mostly since Isobel's death I've been very lonely. I want to talk about Isobel because it's my way of keeping her spirit alive, but I think it makes most people feel uncomfortable. On the one hand, I have never been sadder, but on the other I've never been so struck, as if someone has grabbed me by the shoulders and shaken me, in order to make me think about life. I now know what I want out of life, but I've had to sacrifice my daughter for it. That's what it took to make me a better person.

I am astounded at how much more aware of myself I've become since Isobel died. I want to appreciate the quality of life and start to make the most of every situation. I now realise that death shouldn't just be seen as a negative, because it can show you how to live. Now I know that I would like to be able to help mothers like myself who have lost a child through cancer. I truly admire people who have a gift, and I hope this is mine.

In a strange way, Isobel's death has made me a lot more confident. I'm a tougher person, more independent. I have much stronger views. I know my mind, I know my views and I will voice them. My attitude now is if people don't like what I say or how I think – tough. Before, I would concern myself with what people thought of me, now I don't really care. I've grown up. In fact, I feel I've aged twenty years. I see life from a totally different perspective, and every experience is heightened. When I hear a bird singing, I listen to it, and when I go for a walk I take in all the beauty around me so much more than I did before. Death itself is also magnified for me. When I read in the newspapers about the tragedies that happen to children I truly understand what their parents are going through.

I worry quite a lot about not having a healthy family. I watch the way Emily walks, the way she speaks, constantly looking for signs. I think it's only natural to be neurotic at this stage, as she's nearly the same age as Isobel was when she died. We all take it for granted that a tragedy will never happen to us. One happened to Piers and me, but that doesn't mean we're now immune from tragedy. It's wrong to think that because one of our children died from a brain tumour, it's highly unlikely something that traumatic will ever happen to us again. I can't think that way. If it does happen again then there's another lesson somewhere we have to learn. What it is I do not know.

I never think about Emily's future the way I used to think about Isobel's. I don't wonder who she'll marry, what she'll do with her life, without first thinking: 'If she's alive.' Something like this makes you live day to day. Because we'd made plans, we were far more shocked and traumatised to have them suddenly stopped, to have Isobel's future taken away from us. So although I'm more neurotic in some ways, in others I feel I'm a great deal more relaxed.

I have mixed emotions about the new baby. I expect when I do give birth it will be emotionally traumatic. I'm sure I'll be thinking: 'The last time I did this, Isobel was alive.' In a way I feel guilty. I feel I have to remind everyone that although I'm pregnant again it doesn't mean Isobel is forgotten. Funnily enough, we conceived on or around Isobel's birthday. Of course I'm pleased; I want this baby, but I haven't quite come to grips with it yet. I don't want to be congratulated. I don't want people saying how happy they are for me, how it's the best news they've heard in months. I don't want to hear that. It probably sounds selfish or ungrateful, and I hope people will understand how I'm feeling. I'm sure that I will change in time.

Piers and I have come through Isobel's death, from the awful stay in hospital, to watching her in pain, willing her to die, watching her die, all those awful thoughts and difficulties we had. Now I'm able to think more rationally I understand that Piers' way of helping Isobel was by confronting me. He had to channel his feelings somewhere. Piers seemed to do a tremendous amount of very hard grieving from the moment he realised Isobel was not going to live. He was very intense then, and I think this played a part later. Because he had been able to grieve so intensely he was more able to cope after Isobel died. I didn't really start grieving until after she had died – I simply didn't have time. I didn't even think of her dying. If I had I wouldn't have been as strong as I needed to be for Isobel, or as positive.

I admire and envy any couple who find they can grieve in the same way. For the majority of couples, however, that doesn't happen, and it's important, as we learned, to get professional help. It is normal for recently bereaved parents to assume things about each other; this is a very dangerous habit to get into. It's so important to talk things through, to get things out in the open. If not, you end up assuming different things, because you can't see what the other person is going through. Piers assumed I would begin to not mention Isobel so much after a couple of months. He couldn't understand why I had to go over and over it again. And I assumed that he didn't want to talk about Isobel at all, so therefore I cut myself off from him. Inevitably, we reached a dead end, and at that point we had to force ourselves to talk to each other to correct the assumptions we'd both made.

Piers is far more relaxed now, and I think a far more broadminded person. We are still getting to know each other again. We've managed to survive our problems. Now we can both cope with bringing up Isobel's name without fear of discomfort, aggravation or, in Piers' case, pain. It's not so painful for him now, so he's more able to support me when I'm down. He's the first to jump up and give me a hug when I'm upset. I feel now that I can tell him my innermost thoughts about anything, including my grief, and he will understand. We've come through and can now see a light at the end of the tunnel. We'll never be the way we were, however; we're just rebuilding a different life without Isobel, but knowing that Isobel's spirit is around.

What Piers and I went through was awful, so anything else in life has to better, but I also appreciate that we are very much luckier than some people. That makes you more relaxed, more willing to take every day as it comes. Losing Isobel has made me realise the importance of thinking about why we're here, of trying to be more in tune with oneself and not taking life for granted. I felt that my life wasn't going anywhere before Isobel died. I had no particular passion for anything in life, no interests of my own. Isobel's death has changed that. Both of us now stop and look at the world, and think about what we can do to make it better. Our lives are more meaningful, less superficial.

I'm becoming more aware of myself, like a flower about to bloom. I've been a closed bud all these years, and it's taken Isobel's death to make the flower open up and have a look at the real world as opposed to a fantasy world. The old me was a nothing me. My friends would probably say I was far more fun, but I know I've grown up. Who knows whether I'm a better person or not? All I can hope for is that this book will help someone understand and respond to death in a more positive way. If people were more accustomed to hearing about what happens to people when they die, death would be easier to bear. Now I have this hyper determination, this inner drive. They say it takes a very long time to get to heaven.

Chapter Eleven

It's a very English thing to want to keep your thoughts and opinions to yourself. Before Isobel's death, I was always worried about speaking out of turn, and I stayed quiet about certain subjects. But why on earth should we feel awkward or embarrassed or uncomfortable talking about the death of someone we loved dearly? I don't mention Isobel nearly as much as I used to but when I do mention her, it is nice if others can acknowledge her too. It's not that I want pity. All I want is for other people to know the truth about how I'm feeling. That can't be such a bad thing. It's crazy that the only people who are familiar with bereaved parents are counsellors; family and friends who are closest generally haven't got the foggiest idea what to do, or what to say. Then they wonder why they're being distanced.

Generally speaking the English are not good at being compassionate, at confronting situations or wanting to show or face up to emotions that we all feel in different degrees at times like this. A bereaved person can end up feeling quite isolated. If a bereaved parent doesn't want to talk they will say so, or you will soon know. I don't think so-called 'politeness' is any excuse for people just to back away. I only wish they would bring up Isobel in conversation for a change.

There are a handful of well-known sentences which people use when they're responding to the bereaved.

Somehow we're brought up to believe that these words are the right ones to use: 'Life goes on'; 'You'll get over it'; 'At least you've got other children'; 'At least you've got your husband': 'It's not the end of the world'; 'Things could be worse'. All these sentiments are very unhelpful, and can do more harm than good. If more was written on the subject I'm convinced people wouldn't say these silly things, and the bereaved person would go without a lot of the hurt caused by ignorant and thoughtless responses. We're going through enough pain as it is, without having to cope with other people saying the most callous things, even if they aren't intended to offend.

What people can do is simply offer an ear, partic larly if they haven't got a clue what to say. It's enough to point out that you're around any time there's a need to talk. You don't have to do anymore than that. Just listen, listen, listen, and say anything that is soothing or pampering, rather than judgemental or opinionated. Allowing the bereaved to go on and on talking is doing more good than anything, believe me.

However, not all bereaved people want to talk. Some prefer to suppress their emotions. There's not a lot you can do for a person who wants to bottle up. Unbottling a person is a very slow process, as I found with Piers. As time went on and the initial pain lessened, he found that talking about Isobel was not such a bad thing. In the early months it was Jennie, the liaison sister from Great Ormond Street Hospital, who acted as mediator; with the experience she has had with bereaved parents she was able to coax Piers to talk a little more each time we saw her. She made him think about Isobel, about what he was feeling, and very gradually he began to unwind and talk. He had to listen, regardless of how much he didn't want to. For me, talking is the only way of grieving and facing up to your loss. You never, ever finish talking.

Who should you talk to? Someone who's not going to say too much back – you don't want to be given the wrong advice. Even though they might be with you as a friend, they could say something that does more harm than good. I couldn't talk to Piers for a long time because I got snapped at. He was bottling up so much his natural response was to say, 'Shut up, I don't want to talk about Isobel; you're always talking about Isobel.' Jennie was an easy person to talk to because she was with us right from the beginning. This was despite not having any training in bereavement counselling; it was pure experience that made her say all the right things.

Counselling might not be everyone's cup of tea, but I think for the bereaved it can be a very important part of grieving. Local support groups can be a great source of support to some. There is a lot of community support in Britain, but you have to look for it. (At the end of the book is a Helpful Information section, in which I list addresses and telephone numbers of some support groups.) I found lots of phone numbers through friends of friends; I was lucky. It's nice to know they're there, and I'm sure I will get in touch one day, but in the early days I preferred one-to-one situations. As well as counselling, I also decided to see a psychotherapist once a week. She's not only there for the bereavement and grief counselling, but is able to help with all those other sources of worry, such as how other members of the family and friends are reacting towards me, and why I might be feeling a certain way. A severe shock can throw your whole mind into chaos, and she is very gently sorting mine out. She is someone I know I can always talk to, someone who doesn't get emotionally involved. She is there primarily to listen, and not to give advice. I can scream and shout and cry as much as I wish, and it doesn't matter. Having that outlet is very reassuring. The psychotherapist is not going to heal me; I'm not going to be the person I was before Isobel died, but she is helping me to come to terms with life again, and to understand the sort of feelings I am having. Death has churned up everything in my life – childhood, sex, marriage – and she is dealing with every avenue that grief can go down.

People say it's important to cry when you grieve. But each person is different. It very much depends on how much crying you do normally. I wanted to cry more than I did; I suspect that the reason I didn't cry as much as I wanted to was because my feelings were coming out through talking, and because for the first eight months, I was far too numb to cry. Crying is a release, a release of pain. I think talking is one way of dealing with that pain, but crying and talking go together; you can't rely just on one or the other.

Bereavement is a life-long process. Who knows how I will be feeling in ten or twenty years' time? I don't know. What's important is that other people don't hurry you to get better. It's understandable, of course, that they try; they don't like to see you hurting. But if it was an open flesh wound, they would let me get better because they would be able to see it. Bereavement is like a very bad wound that has to heal very slowly, or progress will be reversed. You do heal but you never forget, and you never lose that longing. The one thing I wouldn't want to do is to forget about Isobel. I feel I have to keep reminding people that this will be my third baby. Already I feel they're thinking this is my second.

Life goes on; I don't begrudge that, but you have to acclimatise to grief. Everyone grieves in their own unique way, and the physical symptoms of grief are many and varied, ranging from extreme hyperactivity through exhaustion to moodiness. You get very, very angry, you snap at people, you're very sensitive to what people say. This is why I always compare it with my pregnancies. Everything becomes very strong, very acute, very potent. Some people might sit at home brooding and wallowing. If that's what you feel like doing, my advice is to go with it. Do what you feel you need to do, what you feel you can handle. Don't be told what to do. Obviously you should listen to doctors or bereavement counsellors, but in my experience I found it was best not to listen to people who were too close to you. Every day, every hour, you never know how you are going to feel. You've got to take every day as it comes and not make any plans.

You don't look ahead, you don't dare: all you can see is a big black tunnel with no light at the end. You may find that your sleep pattern is destroyed, and that concentrating is the most difficult thing in the world. You may experience memory loss, restlessness, bitterness, guilt. You may have aches all over your body, difficulty in breathing or swallowing. Some people suffer from nausea, mood swings, or headaches. Bereavement can trigger off some or all of these symptoms; some people may have all of them, others have just a few. More than anything you feel tired. You might have boundless energy one minute, but feel completely drained the next.

Somehow, of course, most people do come out of the downs. Then you plateau, as if your body is having a rest, as if it's cutting you off from the world a little bit and letting you get on with living. Then you'll have another down. As time goes on the downs will become slightly less acute, less painful, less awful, because you know what to expect. And you will probably come out of them that much more quickly. They become fewer and further between, but when you do have those periods the pain itself is just as strong.

If the outside world were more exposed to the bereaved there might be a better understanding of what people actually go through, and more people might have the confidence to offer help and support. I don't think there can be anything worse than losing someone who means the world to you. Whatever people say, you don't get over it. How can you? The intensity of the pain may lessen, but the ache stays; I imagine the dull ache will stay for the rest of my life.

I realise now that Isobel was never meant to live beyond her second birthday, and accepting this means that I feel absolutely certain there was nothing we could have done. I don't think she was meant to live because her condition was so rare. My way of coping was to understand that she had a purpose in life, which was to teach Piers and me a very valuable lesson about caring and loving another human being. Of course, that's not what I thought when she was first diagnosed. I suppose it took three or four months before I came to that conclusion and when I did, I decided to put my whole belief in Isobel. I told myself that she wasn't just a lost life, but someone rather special, like an angel, who had lives to touch and change, and who then left to change others.

Many people have no faith and it's not my place to try and convince anyone why they should. I would just like to show people how in my experience, faith helped me come to terms with my daughter's death. Everyone copes in different ways. I've coped because my faith has become stronger. I really believe Isobel is with us the whole time now. Sometimes I think it would be nice if we all had return tickets to go up to heaven, see those

who have died, and come back again. But I read somewhere that if we knew where everybody went and what
they were doing, and how wonderful heaven was, we
would all want to go there before our time; that is why
we don't know what happens or what it's like. I like to
think that's true.

I know there are millions of people who do not think
the way I do and I respect that; people are entitled to
their own beliefs. But people should also respect that if
faith helps someone through a tragedy, that is just as
valid. I was so angry to begin with; if I hadn't found my
faith I believe I would have been angry for the rest of
my life. I was furious until someone gave me a book
called *When Bad Things Happen to Good People.* It was written by a rabbi whose own son died of an ageing disease
at the age of twelve. It taught me that God cannot control nature. He can't control what people do. He just
guides them, and that's why there are so many cruel
things in the world. That book helped to change my
way of thinking. I remember thinking: 'I'm sorry, it's
not your fault after all.' It's important for people to
reach some sort of inner peace, to place their tragedy in
a context instead of isolating it and bottling it up. If I'd
felt more able to talk openly I think some of my anger
would have diminished sooner.

I was brought up to believe in God and heaven. As a
family we went to church regularly, but it was automatic
and we took it very much for granted. It held very little
meaning for me. Since Isobel's death my faith has
grown, but I don't go to church as much now. In a way I
feel that I don't need to. I feel He's with me every-
where, that He's inside me, guiding me. In the past I
never really thought about God; now I firmly believe
He's always with you, every second of the day.

I'm surprised by the way I feel, by my faith. If I lived

without faith now it would distress me too much to think that Isobel is simply nowhere. I wonder how bereaved people can cope without a faith. At least faith has enabled me to reach a positive understanding of Isobel's death, and I'm now able to cope with my loss. You have to be able to grasp hold of something. You can't sit there for the rest of your life asking: 'Why?'

The Father's View

The prospect of becoming a father for the first time is full of the challenge of the unknown. Certainly, I was not as sure as Georgiana was that the experience was going to be totally agreeable. Previous encounters with children I had found somewhat disconcerting. They tended to stare at me with an all-knowing gaze, intense and speculative. It was Isobel who taught me that this was symptomatic of an inquisitive and enquiring mind, permanently absorbing details of life around it.

Thus I was totally unprepared for the intensity of feeling I had for Isobel when she arrived in our family, a couple of weeks earlier than we had been expecting. Immediately after the birth Georgiana felt nauseous and I was left holding Isobel. I shall never forget the way in which her enormous blue eyes studied me, as I hoped that I would be up to the challenge of fulfilling the complete trust that radiated from her.

From that moment on I was completely absorbed in Isobel. I watched each stage of her growing up, regretting the fleeting and transitory nature of childhood where changes occur on a daily basis, yet longing for her to grow old enough to talk to me. I got to know her better than most working fathers would know their children at that age when I was convalescing for five weeks after an operation when she was nearly six months old.

Even then I counted myself lucky for the opportunity to spend so much time with her.

In retrospect, I can see that this fascination and joy was the normal byproduct of fatherhood. I have enjoyed and been every bit as intrigued by Emily as she grows up, but obviously there is an enormous novelty factor with your eldest child, as the adventure is new to both of you. This same sense of novelty has arrived with Emily now that she is talking and doing things that Isobel never could.

The first ill wind blew one or two months before Isobel went into hospital. I cannot satisfactorily explain why, but when I was playing with her one day in the nursery I was suddenly assailed by an acute sense of loss, and left with a deep feeling of foreboding. It was as if something inside Isobel had broken irreparably, but undetectably. Looking at her I could see only a happy little girl, but try as I might to ignore it, this feeling chilled me for some days. Perhaps my subconscious had picked up signs that my conscious mind overlooked and discounted. It was true that at that stage she was not talking as she should, but we had been told not to worry as children all develop at different rates.

Looking back at photographs of that summer it is so easy now to see how ill Isobel appeared at times. One photograph in particular shows her looking pale, one side of her face slack and her leg and arm positioned unnaturally. I have asked myself so often why we did not see it then, but change creeps up gradually, and without a dramatic difference you cannot see it.

From the moment Isobel entered Barnet General Hospital I was full of foreboding. I could not think of a minor ailment that could have caused her symptoms. Neither, it appeared, could Isobel's GP. Dr Boodle

made only a vague reference to a problem in the cere-
bellum, rather than making light of the matter by saying that it was probably some infection that could be
easily cured. With these thoughts at the forefront of my
mind, the initial diagnosis came only as confirmation of
my worst fears rather than the unexpected shock that it
gave Georgiana.

I had been dreading the diagnosis all day; my job
then had a slight medical slant, which meant that I
knew roughly the size of the problem we were up
against. Naturally I still hoped that it might have turned
out to be a viral infection or similar, but in my heart I
knew that a problem in Isobel's head was unlikely to be
minor; the speed at which she was whisked through the
departments within the hospital only served to under-
line the urgent nature (and thus the severity) of the sus-
pected nature of the problem. Dr Boodle later told us
that her heart sank as soon as she saw Isobel for the first
time, as she felt reasonably certain that a brain tumour
was the root cause of the symptoms. Apparently, a general practitioner normally sees only one child with a
brain tumour in their career; Dr Boodle had just begun
in general practice, and could not believe that it could
happen to her so soon.

We were then launched into a series of battles, each
of which we had to win in order to progress to the next.
In large part I found the stamina to keep going flat out
by concentrating all my energy on the next hurdle without looking beyond it. Our first hurdle was obtaining
admission to Great Ormond Street Hospital. Once in
Great Ormond Street, the second hurdle was to get a
priority position on the waiting list for the MRI scanner.
This carried on focusing our attention; along with the
full-time job of caring for Isobel, it gave us little time to
ponder the future.

Parents new to the wards at Great Ormond Street are easily identified by the disorientated and emotional state from which they suffer for the first few days. In that state I wondered where we would find strength sufficient not to fail Isobel. How aptly a Jewish man, dressed in traditional garb, put it, when he said that we should not worry, as we would find a well of strength inside us that we did not know we possessed until we came to draw on it.

Deep in my heart I knew that Isobel's prognosis was extremely poor after the results from the MRI scan showed a tumour. The quandary I faced was how to remain outwardly positive and optimistic to support Georgiana's enormous determination that Isobel would be cured, when in reality and in spite of myself, I found myself grieving for Isobel in advance of her dying. This should not suggest in any way that I was not completely involved in trying to find a cure. It was more that I approached the crisis with the pragmatic view that is my way, while Georgiana consciously, I think, pushed logic to one side and put her whole being into believing that Isobel would recover. She did this with such intensity that she appeared to believe that the power of belief could cure in itself, but I could not ignore the warnings we were receiving about how difficult it was to do anything with a tumour in the brain stem. Perhaps my losing a brother, who had been roughly the same age as Isobel, had shown me that these tragic events can happen.

In the face of such faith I could not bring myself to share my true thoughts. Nor could I prevent myself from grieving at a time when we were still fighting hard to find a cure. I could not shake off my conviction that Isobel would die, and found myself examining my dashed hopes for her future. She was so intrinsically bound up in my life that I found the anchors of all that I believed in swept away.

Every day when I went to work I went for Isobel, to give her the best life and future that I could. She was the fundamental motivation in my life, and suddenly I had to face the prospect of her being taken away, that she would not be getting married, that all my hopes for her were to be destroyed. Emily was so young and the shock to my system so great, that she could not at that stage replace Isobel as my prime motivator. It took about six months after Isobel died for that to occur, during which time I had enormous motivation problems at work. My subconscious was insistently and illogically telling me that working was pointless in the great scheme of things. Why work and miss out on the children growing up? The terror of another mishap cutting another precious segment out of the family was and still is extremely powerful. Somehow niceties such as how the grocery bills were to be paid were ignored by this inner voice.

In a sense there was no one moment when the final diagnosis was given to us. It was more a gradual process of being made aware of the supreme difficulties that the doctors were encountering. I am certain the slow progress we made towards the realisation that Isobel would die was intentional on behalf of the medical staff. It is quite different to know that the chances of success are slim to being told that your child will definitely die. Depending on the character of the parent concerned, it could be too much of a shock to be told bluntly at the outset how faint the chances really are. However, the signs were there if we looked: one of Isobel's nurses being comforted in tears by a colleague; the pitying looks of other parents; and other smaller discordant notes. Although the diagnosis had not yet been made from her tests, experience had obviously made it plain to the seasoned onlookers that we were hard up against the wall of the impossible.

For me, the moment of finality arrived on an afternoon when Isobel had been in a lot of discomfort, and was not being helped by normal pain killers. Her crying sawed at our nerves: the tumour was irritating her to the extent that she did not know her own mind, and would request one thing after another, never satisfied. The nurses did not want to give her more powerful drugs until they had a better idea of what her tests had concluded.

After a couple of hours a young doctor came to see if she could be given anything stronger for her pain. Having read Isobel's notes and examined her, we were asked to go into an office for a discussion. For the first time in a few hours we were parted from Isobel crying, the quiet of the office like an oasis of peace in the middle of the nightmare that still raged outside. The doctor appeared uncertain how to proceed as, not having been briefed by Isobel's consultant, she was unaware of what we had been told. Feeling that I knew why she was hesitating, I prompted her by asking whether Isobel, in her opinion, would recover. Her reply was direct. Based on the notes, she said she saw few chances of Isobel recovering. She also went on to say, without conviction, that we should not give up hope. All day I had been longing for a frank opinion, but at this, the confirmation of my worst fears, I was frozen to my chair in shock, the doctor's words flowing around me unheeded

I cannot remember leaving the office, just that we decided to go outside on our own to recover before seeing Isobel. We were at one with one another, silent in our pain, moving numbly towards the exit, our world shattered. Within sight of the door we met a couple

who had befriended us on the ward. They asked after
Isobel. My mouth opened and closed, but no noise
would come out. Reading the look in our eyes they suddenly realised what had happened. They said how desperately sorry they were, and that they would find us
later if we wanted to talk. Their support and understanding was an anchor to hold onto. Any embarrass-
ment we might have felt at being found in this state was
completely removed by them saying how they had
encountered us at 'the worst moment of our lives'. How
well that describes it.

It was then that we were to investigate the possibilities
of a course of chemotherapy. In advance of our meet-
ing the specialist to discuss this option, I was haunted
by mental pictures of Isobel looking sick and grey from
the toxic drugs, her eyes pleading the question: 'Why
are you doing this to me?' I was dreading confronting
Georgiana with my reluctance to pursue this course of
action, unless of course the chances were reasonable
that Isobel might be cured. In a strange way, perhaps
because I had so little faith in and was so frightened by
the drugs, when we were told that chemotherapy was
unlikely to have any benefit, I was relieved. I was further
relieved to find that Georgiana had felt the same way as
I had all along and was nervous of sharing her thoughts
with me. We had reached the end of the road, and all
that was left to us was to take Isobel home and make her
as comfortable as we could for what time she had left.
The only remaining uncertainty was how long she had.
Unlike in films, no one could tell us.

At this time I was feeling the most appalling helpless-
ness and the strong underlying, almost subliminal,
undercurrent that I had failed in my simple duty to my
family. I had failed to find the solution to Isobel's prob-

lems. This haunted me, until I sat down and rationalised the emotion. It was misdirected, the result of my encountering, for the first time, something totally unattainable, no matter how much money or hard work was thrown at it. Previously I could not have conceived of a chain of catastrophic events occurring in my family in slow motion that I could not circumvent. How utterly frivolous and pointless the efforts and achievements of my life seemed at that stage. What was the point of having strived so hard for an ideal of insulating my family from some of the dangers that life throws in front of all of us, only to find that the protection was an illusion and did not, in fact, exist?

Likewise the trauma of accepting that the phase of fighting the disease had ended and that the phase of terminal care had begun cannot be understated, as it goes against all the protective instincts that are natural in a parent. An incident that occurred when Isobel came home from hospital highlights this conflict between instinct and common sense. She had been requiring incrementally more and more pain control, and had reached the maximum recommended dosage of her pain killer. The doctor from the hospice had to ask our permission to begin giving Isobel morphine. I asked two questions: Would the drug be addictive? Would it shorten her life? The answers I received were shocking. Yes it was probably addictive, and yes it might shorten her life; but I should consider that at this stage of Isobel's illness drugs should be used for her comfort rather than for any therapeutic benefit, as she was in the last few weeks of her life.

I was immensely fortunate through this period in having an employer who was tremendously understanding and stated, quite simply, that I should go and do what I had to do and to look after the important things

in my life. However, I wonder how many other employ-
ers would be prepared to make that kind of commit-
ment, effectively giving me unlimited time to spend
with my daughter in her last days. I did try to work during that period, but not for long. Part of me longed for
the sense of normality it brought, and part of me
resented it separating me from Isobel.

When you know that one of your loved ones is going to
die in the immediate future it gives the time you spend
with them a special quality. It is akin to a particularly
magical dream, in which the sensations are headily
intoxicating and very vivid, but at the same time you
know that it is going to end shortly when you wake up.
It makes special moments very poignant, and there
were times when the knowledge of impending loss
made the happy moments unbearably sad. I remember
particularly the occasions when Isobel would embrace
Emily and give her the hugely wet kisses that children
of that age deliver. Emily would gurgle contentedly, but
I would feel desperate that she would never really know
her sister. Isobel's tragedy was Emily's tragedy as well.

Another occasion which was bitter-sweet was when
my mother came to see Isobel on a day which turned
out to be one of the last of the good ones. She was given
a beautiful, huge toy tea-pot which was a dolls' house
inside. The joy on Isobel's face when she looked at this
toy was transparent in its radiance. I could feel the
strangest mixture of joy and the bleakest despair at this
sight; why should this delightful, guileless, beautiful
child be denied the chances of life that we all take for
granted?

It is so difficult to describe how you feel when cud-
dling your child in your lap knowing that every last
second brings the end tangibly closer. How can you

express love to a child in that situation without frightening them? All you can do is act normally, be there for them in their moment of need, and hope that the intensity of your love will make itself felt. I sat for hours on end with Isobel on my lap, her half asleep, me suffering from cramp from having sat motionless for so long. I never begrudged the time spent like this; I was so conscious of the mortal challenge she faced, and wished to give her all the support and love she required to face it. It may sound ridiculous that Isobel could have had any inkling of her predicament, but Georgiana and I both felt in the last few weeks that Isobel had gained maturity way beyond her years. She grew up spiritually in the last stages of her illness, and gave no appearance of being disquieted or worried by her disabilities.

We both desperately wanted to be holding Isobel when she died. Yet I realised that in moments of crisis it is Mummy, not Daddy, that small children need. On one occasion Isobel suddenly stopped breathing for a while. I thought the end had come and called Georgiana. When she came it took me all of my will power to pass Isobel to her and could do so only after exercising considerable restraint. Isobel was my child too, and I was overcome by the urge to hug her little body to try to dispel the overload of grief. It was in part the thought that if she was still aware of her surroundings that she would prefer to be with her Mummy that finally made me pass her to Georgiana. Above all else it was Isobel's moment of crisis, nobody else's, and I could not deny her her final comfort, however much I may have wished it to be otherwise.

When Isobel died a part of all of us went with her. Georgiana and I lost a daughter, and Emily her sister. Although Emily was less than four months old she was very much aware that something was terribly wrong; at times she was only happy when she was out of the house. She was also deprived of her mother through this time, as Georgiana was giving all she had to Isobel. But after the funeral Emily proved how much a child can give. Without her happy smiling face and laughter our house would have been very much the poorer.

The silence in the house was palpable and depressing after the funeral, the contrast stark between the bustle and noise created by a toddler and the brooding silence of two people reliving their memories. Each household has noises and characteristics that distinguish it from another, but when a central piece of the mosaic has gone it changes. Getting used to that was a dimension of bereavement for which I was totally unprepared. Embracing the new atmosphere created by Emily, increasingly vibrant as she grew older, was a key part of the healing process. Whilst it is important to come to terms with the past it is essential also to embrace the future, which for me was contained in Emily.

The difficulty of concentrating on the future was one of the main challenges. The feelings of let down and anticlimax always associated with the aftermath of a long and hard project hit us hard at this time, but with none of the glow of success. We had lived for nothing apart from Isobel for those months, but the climax was our ultimate failure to help her. Raising enthusiasm for anything was going to be hard enough anyway without this additional dampener. In many ways I think that it would have been easier if we had had older children into whom we could have thrown ourselves, but Emily was still at the age when she was asleep for most of the day, and left us twiddling our thumbs.

It was after the funeral that the differing way in which

Georgiana and I grieved caused some friction. She wished to talk ceaselessly about Isobel, and I wished to tuck away that part of my emotion in order to deal with and control it properly. There can be no right or wrong in these matters, in my opinion. People should do what feels best for them, but it did cause friction between us as we coped in such diametrically opposing ways. I found it extraordinarily difficult to comfort Georgiana in the months after the funeral. The usual experience of bereavement in a family is of losing a parent, where one spouse can support the other as for one the loss is inevitably less. The death of a child is something that hurts both parents so badly that you are trying your best to cope with your own emotional turmoil, with little hope of understanding and sympathising with the other. I found the subject too painful to discuss, and Georgiana found relief only in discussion. This caused a distancing in our relationship which people have since found surprising. It is not really. Many disasters bring couples closer together, but losing Isobel hurt us so badly and found us at such a stage of exhaustion that neither of us had the emotional capacity nor the stamina to be able to be mutually supportive. The effort of understanding the other's feelings was beyond us at that stage, our own individual hurt too great. It took quite a while before gradually, as the hurt subsided, we began to communicate as before and support one another as one would ordinarily.

I will always count Isobel as part of the family. I am sure she is with us in spirit, just as I always felt that my younger brother, who died aged eighteen months, was always with us and part of our family as I was growing up. Emily will always know she had an elder sister. Now that she is two years old she points at a photograph of

Isobel that hangs on the stairs and says, 'Gone.' In her own way I think she understands, but she does not appear at all worried by it.

My concern is that Emily as she grows up may think that we loved Isobel more than her. I hope that as a sensitive growing girl she can appreciate that it was not an excess of love that made us spend so much time with Isobel, but that Isobel was in need and we would do the same for any of our children. In fact it was our love for Emily that was the important common ground between Georgiana and myself upon which we rebuilt our lives. She was the happy, and much loved, heart of our new household, and her laughter the best therapy for us both.

Looking back now I am surprised by how few regrets I have. Isobel's illness gave us time to say our goodbyes over an extended period of time. In this respect our situation was so much easier than those who lose a child in a sudden accident, with no time to prepare. My regrets are that I wish we had taken her to the beach more often; she loved it there, but only spent one very wet week in Cornwall. I also wish that she could have talked to me, to unlock the secrets of her mind, at which I could only guess while looking into the depths of the expression in her eyes. The most important thing for me was that she died secure in the knowledge of the love and support around her in her home. This having been achieved, other regrets much surely be secondary. I cannot rationalise such a pointless and meaningless end to a joyful and potentially useful life that had hardly begun. However, if by writing this book Georgiana helps someone else, then I believe that Isobel dying will not have been totally without purpose.

I hope also that it has highlighted successfully the tremendous dedication and professionalism of all the medical staff, particularly those from the hospice and Great Ormond Street Hospital. It is hard to describe the simply amazing dedication, understanding and humanity of the staff there. They cope day in day out with very seriously ill children and their parents whilst retaining a great sense of fun. A few mornings when we arrived in the ward we found some of the nurses pushing Isobel up and down the passage at speed in a cardboard box to the sound of peals of laughter from Isobel. She had them wrapped around her little finger as well. I will also be eternally grateful to the team at the North London Hospice, without whose support I am sure Isobel would have died in a hospital. They were always available at short notice, day and night, and I shall always remember them for their quiet efficiency and compassion.

Miracles do occur at Great Ormond Street on an increasingly frequent basis. It is possible to cure leukaemia, depending on what form of the disease a child has; even brain tumours can be cured, although brain-stem tumours such as Isobel's remain very difficult to tackle. Huge advances have been made in recent years, and indeed Isobel herself received some pioneering treatment at one stage which will have given the doctors just that much more experience and data to use when confronting another case. Sadly, Isobel was not to be one of the lucky ones, but with the optimism, skill and sheer drive of the medical staff I can easily believe that many hurdles will soon be overcome.

I have changed as a person as a result of losing Isobel. When she became ill I realised how much in life I had taken for granted, and how much of what I regarded as important was not. Georgiana's faith has been strengthened since Isobel died, mine I find unchanged. Good and evil appear much the same to me now as they did then, but it has underlined that people are the most important things in our lives. Too often I think the stresses of modern life mask that basic truth, and it took this tragedy to make me understand how reversed my priorities really were. Quality of life is too often forgotten. I am looking forward to Georgiana having another baby; and I am determined to spend enough time at home so as not to run the risk of saying that I will do something tomorrow only to find that tomorrow is not there.

Afterword

I got to know the Monckton family through my work as a neurosurgical liaison sister at Great Ormond Street Hospital; I was involved in caring for Isobel and supporting the Moncktons from her diagnosis until a year after her death. My contribution to *Dear Isobel* is based on my experiences of working with children and their families where a diagnosis of a brain or spinal cord tumour had been made. My work involved coordinating the child's treatment and care, and providing emotional support and practical advice to the children and their families. I also worked alongside community teams when a child needed home nursing, and continued to care for families when a child was dying. Ongoing support was offered to bereaved families for as long as they needed it.

When a child is diagnosed with a serious illness the shock can leave parents reeling. Treatments can take months or even years before it is known whether they have produced a cure. Illnesses can be short or long lasting, with fluctuations between good and bad health. At the time when a child's illness becomes impossible to cure, medical management moves into a new phase based around controlling the symptoms, with an emphasis on the best quality of life possible. It is very unlikely that an exact time span can be given for a child's life. At all stages of an illness there are often choices associated with the medical management and care of the child, and it is vital that parents recognise their right to be fully involved in all the decisions that have to be made.

Caring for a child whose future is uncertain is hugely

demanding physically and emotionally. Every child is unique, and it is impossible to set out a fixed pattern of events. Parents have a right to provide for their child in the way they feel is best for the whole family, and children can be cared for in hospital or at home. In some areas there are special children's hospices, or special facilities in some general hospices. Hospital staff and the family GP will have information on what local services are available to help the family care for the child as they wish to. Families will always be able to receive medical and practical advice wherever they are. Parents should feel free to discuss their fears and needs with those caring for them, and should never feel that they are wasting medical staff time or that they should stop questioning or asking for help.

Children too have the desire to talk about their illness. This very often includes a need to talk about dying which many adults find hard to deal with. However difficult this may be for parents, the child has a right to know what is happening. It is staggering how children approach their illness and dying with a maturity and wisdom far beyond their years. Not every child will want to talk, but for those who do it is wrong to deny them the opportunity; the professional team involved with the child's care will be able to offer advice and support.

Georgiana and Piers have written very movingly about the time leading up to Isobel's death. I will concentrate on what may happen to a family in the aftermath of a child's death. I hope that what I have to say may be helpful for both bereaved families and those who are supporting them. For each family that experience will be different in some respects. No two griefs are the same, and what follows here is based on what I have learned from many different people.

There is no right or wrong way to grieve for a child,

just as there is no right or wrong way to bring up a child. Likewise there is no defined timetable of events through which people pass. Unfortunately, people who have not been through the ordeal themselves sometimes give well-meaning but inappropriate advice, which can be very difficult for a grieving parent to deal with. Parents need to be allowed to do and say what they feel is right for them, and not to be swayed into doing or feeling something against their judgement. For family and friends the most valuable support that can be given to bereaved parents is to allow them to mourn in their own way.

It is very hard to be a supporter of bereaved parents. The biggest tendency, and one I continue to battle against, is to try to 'make it better' for the grieving mother or father, as it is a natural instinct to want to relieve someone's suffering. In the case of bereavement, however, not only is it impossible to take the pain away, it is inadvisable. Parents need to acknowledge and face up to the pain in order to come through it. Avoiding it does not help, because in the long run it will reappear, even if the painful feelings are buried for months or even years. The intense pain will eventually change and ease, but more often in years than weeks or months.

Each person deals with the death of their child in their own way, as Piers and Georgiana illustrate. Most partners will not previously have faced such a traumatic experience together. In one sense grieving is inward looking, and when two people are grieving the same loss it is impossible to provide adequate sympathy and understanding for the other. It is hard to understand and accept that one person deals with their emotions in a way which is totally different and possibly unacceptable to the other. Friction is almost certain to occur, not least because following the death of a child you are physically and emotionally exhausted. Often one partner is scared to say something which may make the other feel worse than they already do. Sharing feelings with each other and not being judgemental can be invaluable for bereaved couples. Be prepared to listen, but don't expect too much from each other. If problems are ongoing, outside help may be useful (see Useful Information at the end of the book).

I am aware that the focus here is on couples. It is even harder for a single parent, who may have no one close with whom to share the pain and grief. It is especially important that these people are provided with the support of a group or helper, and friends need to be particularly aware of and sensitive to the needs of such vulnerable parents.

Grieving is a necessity, not a weakness. It can include many different thoughts, feelings and responses which change from day to day and hour to hour. This is not only frightening and exhausting for the mourner, but also difficult for supporters to understand. Grief shows itself in a range of ways, from lethargy to hyperactivity, exhaustion to insomnia. There are times when it seems the tears will never stop and others when they just won't come. Emotions can become desperately confused, or even vanish altogether. Forgetfulness and absentmindedness are common; some people say they feel they are going mad. Feelings of isolation and the desire to speak to anybody and everybody coexist with the need for time and space alone. Guilt occurs when feelings of happiness begin to reappear, but it is important to understand that laughter is as natural as tears.

After a child has died there is an intense yearning to see, hold, hear that child again, and some people find comfort in the smell of the child's clothing or taking a favourite toy to bed with them. Sometimes feelings of anger are directed at the dead child for leaving and causing so much pain. Memories seem to work backwards from the time of death, so that initially the only memories are of the child ill or dying. Gradually, as each painful time in the child's life is thought through, the happy and positive memories begin to return, and stay.

Parents also find that there are times when it is impossible to recall the child's face or voice, or else memories seem to fluctuate between indistinct images and ones of pure clarity. One of the most difficult things to face is when thoughts of the child do not occupy every second of the day. This can cause feelings of disloyalty, but children are not loved any less if they are not continually being thought about, and this is also true of a child who has died.

Often the bereaved are avoided completely, and another common concern for grieving parents is when family and friends are reluctant to mention the dead child's name. Each parent has to find their own way to deal with these situations.

For friends and family knowing the right things to say and do seems almost impossible. What is a helpful comment one moment is totally wrong the next. If it seems that there are just no words that sound right, it is better to say so than to say nothing. Reminiscing is good, but it is also essential that grieving parents think about their present feelings concerning the child. One of the most important functions of a friend is to be a sounding board for grief, whether through listening or through sharing silence.

Much has been said about parents, but what about other children in the family who are alive and well?

Brothers and sisters are not only sad but confused about their feelings and the behaviour of the adults around them. Children often grieve in a different way to adults. Periods of intense sadness mingle with times of happy activity; behaviour changes and mood swings may occur. They sometimes take on the responsibility of trying to cheer adults up, or trying to replace the child who has died by taking on some of the qualities of their sibling. These children have questions and guilt feelings too, but may think they should not or cannot talk about them. Some children feel very left out, and can suffer from thinking the dead child was perfect whilst they are inadequate in their parents' eyes.

Siblings should be encouraged to be involved in any discussions concerning their brother or sister if they wish it, and offered the opportunity to share their own feelings. Children often want to attend the funeral, which should be encouraged; many children who are not allowed to do so bitterly regret it later on. It is quite normal for children, especially those who are older, to prefer not to speak in depth with their parents. Involving a relative, teacher or other adult who is close to the child may be necessary to draw them out to talk.

Parents often feel overprotective of their remaining children, and even of each other. The vulnerability of life has been made terribly clear, and it is quite natural to feel like this. As far as possible the remaining children should be allowed to lead their lives normally.

Extended family and close friends also grieve, and need to have their pain and sadness recognised. They not only grieve for the dead child, but experience the pain of seeing and longing to help the suffering of the child's parents. Grandparents especially feel frustration at the unfairness of their grandchild dying while they live on. The extended family very often does not receive the mourning status that would give them time to grieve as they might wish to.

Life for a bereaved parent is totally different. While the world carries on around them, the bereaved are left to deal with each new day without their child. Time looms ahead in a frightening way, so coping with the present and getting through each day can make the future seem slightly less daunting. There can be a tremendous loss of confidence, and for a bereaved parent the simplest of tasks is an achievement. As small steps are taken it will gradually be easier to take more and bigger ones.

Unfortunately our society wants a bereaved family to be 'back to normal' as soon as possible. Being back at work, going on holiday, having another child and so on seems to symbolise to the world that everything is better. It is much easier for everyone else if bereaved parents are fine, but in fact they are not fine and they cannot pretend to be – least of all to themselves.

There are many 'firsts' such as birthdays, Mothers' or Fathers' day, Christmas, holidays and days specifically connected to the child's illness and death, which cannot be avoided and will be hard. The build-up is often much harder than the day itself, however. Once a 'first' is over it does not necessarily make the next time easier, but there is the knowledge that you can come through it. Family and friends who continue to recognise the anniversaries of the child's birthday and death are very comforting. Parents will never forget their child, and it is very precious to know that others have not forgotten either.

On a practical level there is much to face. Sorting out the child's room and possessions is especially daunting. This can be done at any time, and should not be done because others think it should be. It will probably never feel acceptable, but people begin to feel strong enough to try. It is better not to discard or give things away until it feels right to do so, as they cannot be retrieved if there is a change of heart.

You do not 'get over' a death and time does not 'heal'. What happens is that gradually what has happened is assimilated into a bereaved parent's life, the future is reshaped into something different yet meaningful. Not everyone is able to do this by themselves, and there is nothing wrong in seeking help. Local health centres should be able to assist in finding professional guidance, and at the end of the book there is a short list of organisations that may be able to offer help.

Initially the way is bleak; there are no answers and no way out: survival is what is needed. Parents can think back over what has already been 'survived' – the diagnosis, treatment, illness, death. Life continues but in a profoundly changed way, and the past will always influence what lies ahead. I never cease to be amazed at the resilience and bravery of parents who have been bereaved of a child. Over the years they do find a way to live with the tragedy in a way that is meaningful and positive.

Jennie Salkeld
Former Neurosurgical Liaison Sister, Hospital for
Sick Children, Great Ormond Street, London

Helpful Information

There are a number of support groups and organisations that are connected with bereavement, although few that specialise in the loss of a child. Everyone will respond differently and have different needs after a death in the family, but if you think you would like to talk to someone about what is happening to you then you could try those I have listed below. There is nothing wrong with thinking that you might need help. Don't give up if the first time you call you don't find it helpful – you may just have spoken to someone who was not right for you. If you feel that you might benefit from counselling you can speak to your GP about this to begin with.

Child Death Helpline
Tel: 071 829 8685
The helpline operates from 7 pm to 10 pm on Mondays and Thursdays; there is a 24-hour ansaphone on this number outside those hours. The service is run by volunteers, all parents who have suffered the death of a child, and have had some training in talking about bereavement.

National Association of Bereavement Services (NABS)
20 Norton Folgate,
London
E1 6DB
Tel: 071 247 1080
List of specialist bereavement services, including Bereaved Parents' Helpline.

The Compassionate Friends
53 North Street,
Bristol
BS3 1EN
Tel: 0272 539639 (helpline)
Organisation of bereaved parents offering shared experience and series of leaflets.

CRUSE Bereavement Care
126 Sheen Road,
Richmond
Surrey
TW9 1UR
Tel: 081 940 4818
CRUSE provides support for the bereaved through local groups; you can find out your nearest local group by telephoning the above number.

Books

As I have said in the book, there were very few books that I found helpful when I went to bookshops to try and find something to read on the death of a child. Since writing the book I have done a little research, and came across one or two more that you might find helpful.

The Death of a Child – A Book for Families by Tess Wilkinson, published by Julia MacRae, Random Century in 1991.
This book has a foreword by Sister Frances Dominica of the hospice for children called Helen House. The first part of the book is for adults, and the second part for children, to help them understand what death is. There are support groups in it, and helpful prayers.

When Bad Things Happen to Good People by Harold Kushner, published by Pan Books in 1982.
As I say in the book, I found this book very helpful in coming to a spiritual understanding of Isobel's death.

A Child's Questions about Death, published by
St Catherine's Hospice, Malthouse Road, Crawley, West Sussex.
Tel: (0293) 547333
This book has a Christian orientation, and may help other children in the family come to terms with what has happened.

Index